THE NOT-SO-SECRET DIARY OF A FOOTBALLER

Ella Toone is an English professional footballer who plays as an attacking midfielder for Women's Super League club Manchester United and the England national team. Born in Tyldesley in Manchester, Ella joined Manchester United's youth academy at 8 years old and has been playing ever since. She became a European champion with the Lionesses in 2022 and scored a crucial quarter-final equalizer against Spain as well as a goal to open the scoring in the final against Germany. Ella's first children's book was *Three Lionesses*, which she wrote with teammates Nikita Parris and Georgia Stanway. It was a bestseller in children's non-fiction.

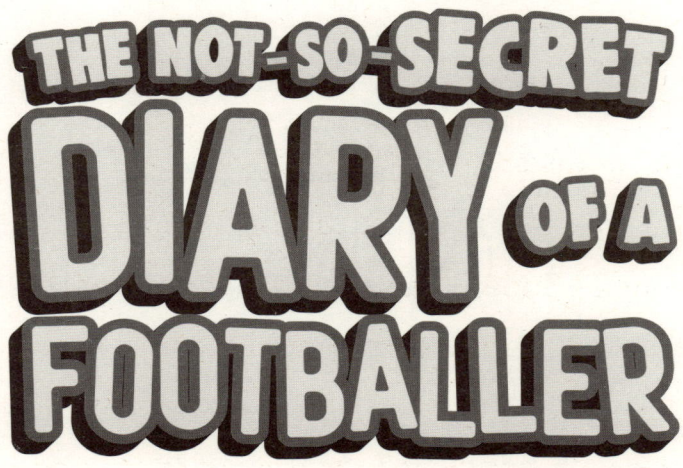

ELLA TOONE

Written with Kay Woodward

PUFFIN

PUFFIN BOOKS

UK | USA | Canada | Ireland | Australia
India | New Zealand | South Africa

Puffin Books is part of the Penguin Random House group of companies
whose addresses can be found at global.penguinrandomhouse.com

www.penguin.co.uk
www.puffin.co.uk
www.ladybird.co.uk

First published 2025
001

Text copyright © Ella Toone, 2025
Text by Kay Woodward
The moral right of the author has been asserted

Penguin Random House values and supports copyright.
Copyright fuels creativity, encourages diverse voices, promotes freedom
of expression and supports a vibrant culture. Thank you for purchasing
an authorized edition of this book and for respecting intellectual property
laws by not reproducing, scanning or distributing any part of it by any
means without permission. You are supporting authors and enabling
Penguin Random House to continue to publish books for everyone.
No part of this book may be used or reproduced in any manner for the
purpose of training artificial intelligence technologies or systems. In accordance
with Article 4(3) of the DSM Directive 2019/790, Penguin Random House
expressly reserves this work from the text and data mining exception.

Set in 13/24pt Justus Pro
Typeset by Jouve (UK), Milton Keynes
Printed in Great Britain by Clays Ltd, Elcograf S.p.A.

The authorized representative in the EEA is Penguin Random House Ireland,
Morrison Chambers, 32 Nassau Street, Dublin D02 YH68

A CIP catalogue record for this book is available from the British Library

ISBN: 978-0-241-77158-7

All correspondence to:
Puffin Books
Penguin Random House Children's
One Embassy Gardens, 8 Viaduct Gardens, London SW11 7BW

Penguin Random House is committed to a
sustainable future for our business, our readers
and our planet. This book is made from Forest
Stewardship Council® certified paper.

This book is dedicated to my Dad, Nick Toone x

THE NOT-SO-SECRET DIARY OF A FOOTBALLER

THE BIT AT THE BEGINNING WHERE I EXPLAIN EVERYTHING

Don't panic! I'm not going to explain ABSOLUTELY everything here. If you're hoping for a mind-blowing discussion about how the universe began or what the point of algebra actually is or why grown-ups get quite so obsessed about bin day, then you definitely *haven't* come to the right place. Instead, what I AM going to do is explain why I'm writing this diary.

You see, the Lionesses are heading into a big football tournament right now. And when I say big, I mean BIG. I'm stupidly excited, but I'm nervous too. So the England manager came up

with a sick idea – she reckons that keeping a diary is the perfect way to settle my nerves. According to her, writing stuff down is a great way of de-stressing, and it'll help me to be totally zen on the pitch.

I LOVE this idea. ♡

But while I know that normally a diary is meant to be totally top secret, what I think is an even better plan is to share my scribbles with YOU. I know just how incredibly lucky I am to be an actual Lioness, and so, rather than keep it all to myself, I'd like to let you know what it's really like to be a footballer. (*Psst* – you might even be inspired to become a player yourself in the not-too-distant future!)

So, here's what I'm going to do. I'm going to write

THE NOT-SO-SECRET DIARY OF A FOOTBALLER

down EXACTLY what goes down behind the scenes. I'll talk about all the feels I get in the build-up to a match and a tournament, and what it was like to WIN THE EUROS. I'll squeeze in a load of flashbacks because I have too many amazing memories to keep them to myself, and it's good to share. And I'll tell you about all the hilarious stuff that happens off the pitch – in the changing rooms, at training camps and SO MUCH MORE. It'll ALL be there – the highs, the lows and the funny bits in between that don't make the headlines. And goals. Don't forget about the **gooooooooaaaaaaaaals!**

So whether you're an aspiring footballer who gets covered in mud every Saturday morning, or you love cheering your favourite team on from the stands (it'd better be Manchester United or the Lionesses!), or you're just starting to discover how

ELLA TOONE

fun football can be, this is for you. Get ready to find out what really happens behind the scenes AND on the world stage in my not-so-secret diary.

Tooney

THE NOT-SO-SECRET DIARY OF A FOOTBALLER

ME, ME, ME

Training for the tournament kicks off (see what I did there?) in a couple of weeks, so before the mayhem starts, I'm going to take this opportunity to tell you a bit about myself. I mean, let's be honest – if you've seen the name on the cover of this lovely shiny book, picked it up, bought it AND reached page 5, the chances are that you probably know who I am already, but you might not know the WHOLE backstory. So here goes.

I'm Ella Toone. I'm a professional footballer with Manchester United FC AND I'm one of the Lionesses.

There, I said it. I still can't believe how ridiculous that sounds. I'd pinch myself if it didn't hurt. The fact that I play professional football for ACTUAL Manchester United in the ACTUAL Women's

ELLA TOONE

Super League, and I'm one of (deeeeeeep breath) the ACTUAL England squad, which makes me an ACTUAL Lioness, still hasn't properly sunk in, even though it's been quite a while now. But it is true!

My family calls me Ella, because that's my name. And my mum calls me Ella-Bella, which I love. (I'm NEVER Tooney at home. Think about it – when loads of us share the same surname, it would get MEGA confusing if we all had the same nickname.) But when it comes to football, EVERYONE calls me Tooney. Maybe because it sounds a bit cooler when it's yelled at a gazillion decibels across a football pitch. Like this:

TOOOOONEY!

See?

When I was much younger, I played for Astley & Tyldesley FC, then Manchester United (whoop!). Blackburn Rovers FC was next, before Manchester City FC and then it was just a short hop across town, back to my beloved Manchester United. At the same time, I was going through the ranks with England, playing for them as an under-17, under-19 and under-21 before hitting the big time in the senior squad.

ELLA TOONE

Here are some stats and facts about me!

	MANCHESTER UNITED	**THE LIONESSES**
Position	Midfielder	Midfielder
Debut	19 August 2018	23 February 2021
Jersey number	7	10

That's the same number jersey that Cristiano Ronaldo wore when he played for Manchester United. And David Beckham. Just saying.

My legacy number is 216, which means that I'm the 216th player to be called up to join the Lionesses.

Three guesses what my favourite position is . . .?

THE NOT-SO-SECRET DIARY OF A FOOTBALLER

Is being a footballer the best gig in the whole world? I can answer that in less time than it takes to chip in an equalizer. YES. Yes, it is. Football is so much more than a few people just kicking a ball around – it's a game filled with skill, speed, agility, thrilling passes, near misses and raw emotion. (It's obviously filled with quite a lot more, but there are over 200 pages in this diary, so I'd better save SOME of the good stuff for later on.) Football might be awesome to watch, but I can exclusively reveal that being part of it is nothing short of INCREDIBLE. Don't get me wrong; it's hard work too. But without the graft, you wouldn't get the magic, would you?

There's one more thing that I love about football: it's a game that you play WITH YOUR BEST FRIENDS. And believe me, it doesn't get better than that.

ELLA TOONE

MY FAVOURITE PLACE IN THE ENTIRE WORLD

I banged on enough about myself yesterday, so today let me tell you about my hometown. Ahhhhh, Tyldesley... It's tricky to spell, a bit of a mouthful to say and has far too many consonants for its own good. If you know it, you'll likely call it *Til-slee* instead, which is WAY easier.

Tyldesley is quaint and small. It's in the north-west of England very near Manchester (otherwise known as Manchestahhhh), which I'm reasonably sure you WILL have heard of. Tyldesley is where my family is. It's where my friends live. I love it. I love everything about it. I can't see myself living anywhere else. If I ever moved, I'd always come back to Tyldesley because it's just HOME.

Now, on to Manchester. As well as being a totally cool city with a massive club scene and red-brick backstreets where they film a LOT of TV dramas, Manchester is famous for its two world-class football clubs – Manchester City and Manchester United – as well as a bunch of other local teams. As a result, I've been surrounded by football for ever. It's basically in my blood.

GOING BACK TO MY GRASSROOTS

This morning, I drove past Astley & Tyldesley. That's the first club I EVER played for. You know that feeling you get when you see a place and it reminds you of a really special and happy time in your life? Maybe it's a park that you spent long summer days playing in when you were younger. Or a relative's house that's filled with memories of noisy family meals and building pillow forts between the sofas. That's what Astley & Tyldesley does for me. When I saw the grounds today, SO many unforgettable memories flooded back.

Perhaps my number-one memory is being scouted. This is basically when football experts spot players who they believe have the potential to go on to become professional players and then fast-track them on to a training programme. Players don't have to be brilliant already to be scouted. They just have to play as if, with proper training, they could be **AWESOME.**

One of my coaches, Lee Povah (who I now owe BIG TIME), spotted that I could kick a ball reasonably well. So when I was about seven, he asked a scout called Kat Beaver to come down to Astley & Tyldesley to see how I played. Kat (who I also have SO MUCH to thank for) did, and must have thought that I showed promise. And because she knew someone who worked at Manchester United, I got the chance to try out at the Manchester United Centre of Excellence*. I went for a six-week trial and, after two weeks, they wanted to sign me. The rest – as they say – is history!

My mum always says, 'Never forget where you're from, Ella.' And I don't. I was four or five when I

---

* This is a brilliant youth academy that helps younger players to be the best they can be. They have such a cool programme: intensive training, fitness tests, the chance to play against other great teams, you name it.

ELLA TOONE

joined the Astley & Tyldesley Girls team. And if it wasn't for them, well . . . I wouldn't be where I am today. My very first club has an incredibly special place in my heart.

I'm so grateful to all the teams I've played for, who have done SO much for me. And that's why I wanted to do something to give back to my local community. In 2024, I launched the ET7 Academy to give girls a chance to kickstart their own footballing dreams and learn important skills both on and off the pitch. Just think, there might be future England players just waiting to be discovered, who start out at the ET7 Academy . . .

MY DREAM TEAM (THAT'S MANCHESTER UNITED, IN CASE YOU'VE JUST ARRIVED FROM MARS)

I. Am. So. Lucky.

I've just told myself this in the bathroom mirror, and it's something I remind myself of about a bazillion times a day because it's true. Let's take a look at the facts:

1. I grew up supporting Manchester United, watching the team play with my family.

2. Now I'm playing for Manchester United MYSELF in their first-ever women's team.

ELLA TOONE

If that's not living the dream, what is?!

So, anyway. I'm at the Manchester United stadium, Old Trafford, today, waiting to see one of our physios. Short for 'physiotherapists', these are the amazing people who help us to recover from injuries (and to avoid new ones). But instead of just gazing at all the trophies lining the walls, I've brought this diary and a pen. So while I'm here, I'm going to do what my nan says and take a trip down memory lane.

I got my first taste of what it's like to play at Old Trafford way back when I was at the youth academy. I must've been about seven. It was a match day, and it was Manchester United versus Bolton Wanderers FC. And it was truly UNREAL.

When the half-time whistle blew, I was one of the younger players lucky enough to run on to the

THE NOT-SO-SECRET DIARY OF A FOOTBALLER

OLD TRAFFORD PITCH and play five-a-side IN FRONT OF THE RED DEVILS* FANS. Whoa. It was A-W-E-S-O-M-E. As we sprinted out of the tunnel, the noise of the crowd hit us from all sides, like the best cinema surround sound EVER. I remember the exact feel of the grass beneath my feet (lush, smooth, firm yet bouncy – a carpet of green loveliness) and being totally wowed by the fact that, after years and years of watching matches at Old Trafford, I was actually playing there. I've no idea of the score or how well I did. I just know that I was absolutely buzzing to be there!

Don't tell anyone, but I kept a bit of grass as a memento. (It died, but my dreams didn't.)

---

* If you don't support Manchester United (yet), then this is the nickname for Man U.

ELLA TOONE

LESS IS MORE

I saw my best mate today. She was in town for the day, so we went for coffee, or rather *she* did. She got something fancy that ended in O – cappuccino, espresso or something-similar-o. She does have a solid excuse for liking coffee. Her grandparents are from Sicily, which means she's pretty much Italian, even if she was born in Kent. So coffee runs in her veins. I, on the other hand, detest coffee with all my soul, so I had hot chocolate instead, which has the massive advantage of not tasting as if it's made from burnt twigs.

Time for a proper introduction!

My best mate's birth certificate says **Alessia Mia Teresa Russo**. I love how many names she has. But

THE NOT-SO-SECRET DIARY OF A FOOTBALLER

I can't call her that all the time because there would be no time left to say anything else, so it's Lessi or Less for short. Her birthday is 8 February, and she was born the same year as me – 1999. So we're practically the same age. And if you want to guess what she does for a living, here is a small clue . . .

What are the chances?! My best mate is also a footballer! To be fair, who else but another player would listen to me go on and on about scissor kicks and back heels all day? It makes sense, right?

I met Less at training camp* when we were both about twelve years old. At first I wasn't sure if she

---

* I'll bang on about training camps a LOT in this diary, but basically these are where the entire squad goes to stay, to train and practise working together as a team. They are VERY intense and HUGE fun.

even liked me, but she totally denies that. According to Less, as soon as she saw that we were wearing the same type of trainers – but in a different colour – she just knew that we were going to get on. We DID . . . and we STILL do. By now, we've been best friends for over half our lives.

How would I describe Alessia? She's basically THE NICEST PERSON IN THE WORLD. She's caring. She's loving. She's SO fun. Less isn't someone who quietly sits on the sidelines – no matter what's going on, she always wants to get involved. She's got the most amazing sense of humour too and loves to have a laugh. And talking of laughing, have you ever heard her laugh? It's totally infectious. If Less laughs, *everyone* laughs.

Less is someone who's been on the whole footballing rollercoaster with me. We've been

THE NOT-SO-SECRET DIARY OF A FOOTBALLER

through everything together. And she's someone I can always rely on. I totally trust her opinion because she always gives me the best advice. I'd describe her as more than a friend – she's like a sister.

If we're not together, we message all day. If we are together, we talk non-stop. We get on so well that we've even recorded a podcast called *The Tooney & Russo Show* together. Just to warn you, there'll be quite a lot more about Less in this diary, so you'd better get used to her.

A TYPICAL DAY AT UNITED

The England training camp might be right around the corner, but that doesn't mean life at Manchester United hits pause. It's Tuesday today, which is a training day. These all follow the same basic format. And although each session can feel TOTALLY different from the last, here's what a typical day looks like:

7.30 a.m. Leave home. I know, right?! SO EARLY. The traffic gets so bad that this is the time I have to leave in order to be at Old Trafford on time. I'm not good with mornings (this is a MASSIVE understatement, and it's not the last time you'll hear about it), so I can't even bear to tell you when I have to get up to be ready to go at this time.

9.00 a.m. Arrive at Old Trafford. Yep. It takes one and a half hours to get from my house to the club. Thank goodness for podcasts. (I should say that even though I love listening to podcasts, I don't listen to *The Tooney & Russo Show* on my way in. Imagine listening to yourself blabber on!)

9.10 a.m. Get my kit on.

9.20 a.m. BREAKFAST. I always have the same thing – sourdough toast and smashed avocado with fried-*and-flipped* eggs. The flipping is very important. I can't look at a wobbly yolk, especially first thing in the morning. (If I was in America, I suppose I'd say 'eggs over easy', but that's definitely not how we say it in Manchester!) That's all topped off with baked beans. (You can't tell me you're not hungry now just from reading this. Doesn't it sound AMAZING?) Oh, and orange juice. There, that really is it. It takes a LOT of energy to play football.

10.00 a.m. Before I do any training at all, I have a meeting with the coach. This is usually analysis, where we talk about the last match and figure out what went well and what I need to work on.

10.15 a.m. Time for the gym! This is when I do all my exercises. It also warms up my muscles before going out to train.

11.00 a.m. Step out on to the pitch. The session might be an hour to an hour and a half. And the focus is on training and working on things that we've gone over in analysis.

12.30 p.m. DINNER. Shout out to Jimmy the Chef! When he's catering, there's always something incredible to eat. My favourite is probably the pasta.

1.30 p.m. Gym again.

2.30 p.m. Finish with a soak in the hot tub! I spend around fifteen minutes there with the girls, chilling after training. Then I have a shower, get dressed and get back in the car.

4.10 p.m. Home. Ahhhh.

LASAGNE OF CHAMPIONS

I've just eaten tea. (For anyone who's not from the North of England like me, let me explain – I'm not somehow eating a cup of solid tea, because that

ELLA TOONE

would be like something out of a sci-fi film or a cartoon. By 'tea', I mean the meal in the evening that quite a lot of people mistakenly call dinner. Where I live, it's breakfast, dinner and tea.* Try saying it! If nothing else, it's fun confusing people who eat breakfast, lunch and dinner. Thank goodness breakfast is the same – or we'd all be lost. Anyway, I'm waffling. Oops.)

Frankly, if it weren't for my boyfriend, Joe, I'd probably live on chips and curry sauce. And although that sounds totally delicious because I

---

* Because the Lionesses come from all over the country, it's HILARIOUS the number of debates we have at training camp mealtimes over what the meals are *actually* called. You've probably made your own mind up already depending on where you live, so I'm not going to try and change your mind, but here's my super-convincing argument: IT'S BREAKFAST, DINNER AND TEA. Your Honour, I rest my case.

love both*, it doesn't tick ALL the nutritional boxes that a Lioness needs to fuel their body for training. So, Joe has the honour of cooking for us, and I get to eat like a champion. Just FYI, his steak and eggs are SO good. As for the lasagne that we just had for tea . . . it's in the Super League.

SPOOKY SUPERPOWERS

I only saw Less the day before yesterday, but we've messaged about 465 times since then and spoken fourteen times. So it feels like we're never far apart, not really. I sometimes wonder if this is why we've been accused of being telepathic on the pitch . . .

---

* If you've never tried fish-and-chip-shop curry sauce, boy, do you have a treat in store.

ELLA TOONE

We're not, of course. This is a diary, not science fiction.

But it is true that we know each other quite well. So maybe we do subconsciously give clues to each other? Perhaps I crinkle my nose in a weird way that she (correctly) interprets as: *I'm going to feint left, pretend to aim at the goal and then whack it right at you, so you can score instead?* Who knows?*

One of my favourite instances of our telepathic-style playing was during the England match against Northern Ireland on 16 July 2022. After half time, Alex Greenwood, Less and I were all

---

* Just for the record: I don't. I think we just know how each other plays so well that we can anticipate where the other will be and what they'll do next, which is obviously quite handy when you're playing on the same side. But less good if you're not.

subbed on and raring to go. And just three minutes into the second half, Less scored an absolute blinder with her first kick of the match. Just five minutes later, the ball came my way. Now you know in *Star Wars*, when Yoda just *knows* stuff? Well, I just *knew* that Less was near. But, more importantly, it didn't take a Yoda-style sixth sense to work out that she was near the goal too.

I'm not sure if we even made eye contact before I passed her the ball . . . I just tapped it in her direction. Less took possession, made an awesome turn round the defender and then hammered the ball past the goalie and into the net.

THWACK.

It was totally her goal – I was just buzzing to have been in the right place at the right time to get the ball to her. (I officially got an assist though, which was nice.)

But if people want to call us telepathic, no problem. Just imagine if it were true – we'd never need to speak ever again!

THE THEATRE OF DREAMS

I'm back at Old Trafford again for a training day! No matter how many times I go to Manchester United's home ground, I NEVER get bored of it and I never will. It poured down this morning and even through a curtain of rain it looked magical. So, like the rain, this seems like the right moment to shower you with stats and facts about my favourite football ground ever.

THE NOT-SO-SECRET DIARY OF A FOOTBALLER

- Manchester United FC has existed since 1902 . . . and their stadium has been at Old Trafford since 1910.

- There's only one football stadium bigger than Old Trafford in the UK and that's – you've guessed it – Wembley Stadium.

- After Old Trafford was bombed in the Second World War, Manchester United shared a stadium with Manchester City – their rivals on the other side of town – for eight years. (I LOVE this fact. It's just so touching that local rivals would come together in a moment of crisis and share a ground . . .)

- The stadium stands next to Sir Matt Busby Way, a road named after one of Manchester United's longest-serving managers.

- Old Trafford is known as the 'Theatre of Dreams' because – and do excuse me if I go all Shakespearean for a moment – it's as if the players are actors and their game a play, packed with drama and tension, and acted out in front of an audience of (up to) 74,310 people. I think it's fair to say that the dreams belong to both the players and the fans. The name was dreamed up by Sir Bobby Charlton – one of Manchester United's best-ever players and a member of the England team that famously won the World Cup in 1966.

BESIDE MY PEG

It's just a small thing, but I have to share the truly lovely thing that they do for me at Manchester United. My dad died in September 2024, and at

THE NOT-SO-SECRET DIARY OF A FOOTBALLER

Old Trafford they always put a photo of Dad on the wall, next to my peg. I can't put into words how much this means to me, and I always give the photo a kiss before I go out to a game.

MY DREAM PLAYER

I can't quite believe I've reached page 33 in this diary without telling you all about my favourite player EVEERRR yet. So, before we go any further, I need to sort that out.

Ronaldo.

What a guy!

As it's *my* not-so-secret diary, I think I'm allowed to write whatever I like, so do please excuse me while

ELLA TOONE

I just bang on for a moment about my favourite footballer of all time: *Cristiano Ronaldo.*

(Sorry, I just couldn't resist the fancy letters there.)

It's not just me who thinks he's brilliant. Look at the stats!

- Most international goals ever

- First – and so far, only – player to score in five FIFA World Cups

- Most appearances for Portugal

- Portugal's youngest AND oldest goal scorer

- Most Champions League goals ever

THE NOT-SO-SECRET DIARY OF A FOOTBALLER

- ⚽ Manchester United record-holder for the most goals in a Premier League season (2007–2008)

In fact, there are so many more record-breaking stats about Ronaldo that I'd need a bigger diary to squeeze them all in.

I'd absolutely LOVE to tell you all about the time when I bumped into Ronaldo in our local M&S and he invited me round to his house to have dinner with his family and we feasted on the extra-special Portuguese rice pudding with cinnamon sprinkled on top that he and his team eat before every FIFA World Cup match – and he even gave me the recipe! – and then he called up Wayne Rooney and Rio Ferdinand, and we all played football at Old Trafford and he demonstrated the best way to score a goal from the halfway line, and I nutmegged him, and he totally didn't mind, and we signed each other's number-7 jerseys and EVERYTHING . . . (pause for breath) but I can't!

You see, one of my biggest regrets is that I never got to play against Ronaldo, even though we played for Manchester United AT THE SAME TIME (or at least we did until he left in 2022 to play for Al Nassr FC in Saudi Arabia, which is 5,128 kilometres away). In fact, the sad truth is that not only did I never play against Ronaldo, I never even met him. Sob! I used to dream up scenarios where I would arrive at training and be told that we'd be practising by playing against the men's team. But the closest I ever got to him was by pressing my nose against the canteen window at Old Trafford (trying not to breathe too hard, because if I fogged up the glass then I wouldn't see him at all) and spotting him in the car park, where he was walking to his car. It was so nearly a magical moment!

Ronaldo, if you're reading this, Mondays or Thursdays are best for me. Let's meet for coffee and you can finally share all those top tips! Or rather, you can get a coffee. I'll drink something that actually tastes nice . . .

MY ALL-TIME HERO

I was admiring the Manchester United trophy cabinet this morning, as you do. If you've never been to see it, it's a bit like visiting the Tower of London and being dazzled by the Crown Jewels. Except more sporty. And better, obvs. So if you get a chance to visit, go and see it! And while you're in there, check out the 2024 Women's FA Cup trophy. Doesn't that sound lovely? In fact, do you mind if I write it again and put it in bigger letters?

THE 2024 WOMEN'S FA CUP TROPHY.

WE WON THAT. And I might be the tiniest bit biased, but I think this particular trophy is just a little shinier than all the rest . . .

I'm waffling. Back to the point – I'd like to take a moment to talk about probably THE most amazing footballing icon I've ever met. A person who helped Manchester United to win Quite A Few of those trophies. And when I say Quite A Few, what I actually mean is SHEDLOADS. Which, to be precise, is THIRTY-EIGHT TROPHIES.

I never thought I'd have the chance to meet him, but now I have. MORE THAN ONCE. A few times, actually.

SIR ALEX FERGUSON.

Every time I speak to him, I'm just in awe. I grew up watching Manchester United when he was the manager. They'd win everything, and he was the reason I fell in love with the club. I still have to pinch myself sometimes when I remember that I've sat next to him at games and even spoken to him a few times. All I can say is that he's an amazing man (as well as being the greatest club manager of all time, of course).

Chatting to Fergie (I think I'm allowed to call him that) is AMAZING. I first met him in person when he came and spoke to the team before we played a match against Arsenal FC. I would like to say that I listened, nodded thoughtfully at the right bits and made some clever comments like a pundit on *Match of the Day* . . . but the truth is that I just stared at him with my mouth wide open in disbelief that he was really there. (Just imagine a very hungry cod and that was basically me.) But my excuse is that Fergie's such a nice person that every time he speaks, you don't want to interrupt. You just want to listen to every magical word.

Want to know the REALLY cool bit? I've got his number on my phone. Sick, right?

I haven't ever phoned or messaged him though. I'm not sure what I'd say!

THE NOT-SO-SECRET DIARY OF A FOOTBALLER

> **Ella**
>
> Hi, Sir Alex! It's Ella. Ella Toone? Tooney? Number 7? Scored a few goals for Manchester United? And England? Won the Euros in 2022? Brought football home? The one who generally just looks starstruck whenever you appear? Anyway, hi! I was thinking of having a few friends over for crisps and sausage rolls and I'd LOVE it if you could come!

NEXT-GEN FOOTBALLERS

When I was growing up, I'd watch Kelly Smith and Jill Scott and Ellen White and so many other great footballers play, and just DREAM of being like them one day. I desperately wanted to be a footballer, but sometimes I wondered if I'd ever get the chance to play professionally, as even ten years ago, women's football wasn't as big as it is now. It didn't get anywhere near as much publicity as men's football and people just didn't seem to talk about it as much. Seeing women who DID play was so inspirational for me, and I know they inspired so many other young girls to get involved in football too, and to try and achieve their dreams.

Now it's come full circle. One of the most surreal parts of my job is that I get to show younger players what the future might hold for them. So before a tournament, when the nation is talking about women's football and there's loads of coverage on TV and in the news, I appear at a stack of events, both to promote the women's game and to empower the next generation of players.

Today is one of those days, and I CAN'T WAIT. What if I inspire a future Lioness TODAY? What if

I'm the reason they decide to come to a match that changes their life and makes THEM decide to be a footballer? I guess that would make me an actual role model! Me! Ha!

Seriously though . . . I would be so, so proud.

CONFESSIONS OF A USELESS SHOPPER

I've been invited to an awards dinner* and it's tonight! This is seriously one of the best bits about being a Lioness. I love it. Whenever I get offered

---

* If you're wondering what awards dinners are, it's all in the name – they're just fancy dinners where people are given awards! There's usually a stage or a podium at the front and once we've all eaten (the food is awesome by the way) there are prizes given out and speeches, and everyone does a whole lot of clapping.

an opportunity to go to one of these fancy events I think, *Why not?* So I try to say yes to as many as possible. I mean, what's not to like? Apart from anything else, it's nice to get the chance to dress up and not *always* be in a footie kit.

The problem is that I am R-U-B-B-I-S-H at shopping for clothes to wear to these things. I know they will be filled with people taking photos that could end up splashed all over the internet and social media, so it's not as if I can rock up in something that's been in the wardrobe since 2020.

When it comes to dresses, I know that if I buy one, I want it to be comfortable. I'm not saying that I want to dress in a big, baggy sack, but it's not much fun sitting for four hours in a dress that feels like a straitjacket, no matter how amazing it looks. So I know I like comfy, but that's ALL I know.

THE NOT-SO-SECRET DIARY OF A FOOTBALLER

I'd like to be one of those people who's a bit different and quirky with their clothes. Someone who sets trends and has fashion editors writing gushing articles about their dress sense, but I'm just not confident enough to choose these clothes myself. So I admit it – when I go out to events like this, I usually get someone else who's much better at this sort of thing to help.

Confession time . . . I have a stylist. I mean, how mad is that? Next I'll be telling you that I have a butler! (I don't.) Anyway, she's called Crystal and she's awesome. If there's a really big do, she makes me look good!

Then there's my mum too! She LOVES picking outfits for me and she's dead good at it! Her opinions and advice are spot on. She'll be honest about what does and doesn't suit me, and before

ELLA TOONE

I go out, I always show her what I'm going to wear.

And then there are my friends. Sometimes if I'm going out, I borrow clothes from my mates. In fact, we all share each other's outfits when we need to.

So I've got a few lovely people who look after me and help me look my best at events, while I stick to what I'm best at – football.

THE BEST AWARDS, EVER

> **Ella**
>
> Less! HOW sick were the FIFA 11 Awards last night?!

THE NOT-SO-SECRET DIARY OF A FOOTBALLER

Alessia

SO GOOD! I mean, I've met a lot of cool people at the events that I've been to, but FIFA 11 was one of the best EVER. I can't believe how many amazing footballers were there . . . absolute legends of the game!

Ella

Joe was in his absolute element. Usually, I would NEVER ask anyone for a photo and neither would he. But he was like, 'Ella, I CANNOT miss out on this opportunity – my childhood idol is IN THE ROOM.' So he only went and spoke to R9 and got a selfie with him! Actual Brazilian football legend Ronaldo Nazário!!! It was AMAZING.

> **Alessia**
>
> What are you going on about, you doughnut?!
>
> Don't you think there was something JUST A LITTLE BIT BETTER that happened last night . . .?
>
> Like you being named one of the FIFPRO Women's World Eleven at The Best FIFA Football Awards! Now THAT is amazing, mate.

IT'S MY BIRTHDAY!

Happy birthday to ME.

I was born on 2 September 1999. Yeah, yeah – I know. The 90s?! SO last century. Anyway, it should be pretty easy to work out how old I am from that, so I'll let you do the maths.

Anyway, I LOVE my birthday.

It's not because I love being the centre of attention, because I don't. (To be fair, it might look like I do, what with playing in front of up to 74,310 spectators on any given Sunday, but that's really not the case. I'm there to play football. End of.)

And I don't love my birthday just because I might be showered with gifts and have 'Happy Birthday to You' sung to me a bazillion times. (Though once or twice, or maybe even three times, is perfectly acceptable, ta. And if I happen to unwrap a couple of scented candles, then I don't mind that either. Lush.)

Nah, it's because my birthday is the perfect excuse to go out for a meal with my family. And then with friends. Or both together.

ELLA TOONE

That's what I love. And *that's* what I'll be doing tonight.

(OK, FINE. If you want to buy me a birthday gift, I really do love a scented candle. I like to keep them FOR EVER.)

AN ODE TO WEMBLEY

I've come to London on the train today to record a podcast episode with Less! (I'll write more about our podcast properly when I have time tomorrow, but it is SO MUCH FUN. We just witter on and it doesn't feel like work at all!) Anyway, Less and I were in this taxi going across town when I suddenly saw Wembley's iconic arch hovering above the rooftops . . . and instantly hurtled back in time.

THE NOT-SO-SECRET DIARY OF A FOOTBALLER

It was way back – 23 October 2021, to be precise – but it feels like just yesterday that I stepped out on to the pitch at Wembley for the very first time.

Like, WOW.

England's national football stadium was – and still is – mind-blowing. Whenever you play there, it's an honour. Wembley Stadium is where every England player wants to play and every England fan wants to be. I will never get bored of playing there – not even if I live to be 105.

I'll also never get bored of that arch. And talking of that arch, did you know . . . ?

1. Wembley's arch is not just designed to look good – it's holding the roof up too.

2. It's the longest single-span roof arch IN THE WORLD.

3. The roof can be partially closed to keep every single seat in the stadium dry (as long as all raindrops fall straight down).

4. If it rains, the players DO get wet.

PRETTY MUCH THE NICEST THING THAT ANYONE HAS EVER DONE FOR ME, EVER

I'm so touched by some of the thoughtful things that people do. You're not going to believe what happened to me today. There I was in this cafe, waiting to go into the TV studio to record the podcast, and I was moaning on and on to Less about orange juice and how I hate when it has those bits in it. I was totally unaware that I was actually being DEAD LOUD.

Then this lad who worked at the cafe came over to me and said that he was sorry that he'd overheard my conversation (frankly, unless he'd been living on the Moon, he couldn't have ignored me and my foghorn voice, so absolutely no apology was necessary). And then this kind, lovely guy said that he'd got me some more orange juice. (Which was pretty nice already, never mind whether there were bits in it or not.) But then he told me that he'd SIEVED ALL THE BITS OUT. Every single one.

I was so blown away that I had to write it down.

Thanks, mate.

ELLA TOONE

THE TOONEY & RUSSO SHOW

And just like that, I'm back on the train already . . . in three and a bit hours, I'll be back in Tyldesley! I'm going to make the most of the journey and write all about the podcast.

Awwww, I just love filming* *The Tooney & Russo Show* with Less. We both thought the podcast would be a great idea. I think that everyone who's listened to it has really enjoyed it . . . and we've enjoyed doing it! It's a win-win!

---

* Just so you know, the podcast is recorded so listeners can download the audio version. But it's filmed at the same time too so viewers can watch it online. It's like two shows in one! (Twice as much of me – yikes!)

Vick Hope, who works on it with us, is just THE BEST interviewer. (She's also a TV and radio presenter, an author, a journalist AND an Amnesty International ambassador. Could she BE any cooler?) Vick's so friendly and laid-back that it hardly feels like she's interviewing us at all. We just CHAT about everything – and I mean EVERYTHING. Nothing's off limits.

I've got to be honest – the podcast is actually just an excuse to have a laugh and tell some of our crazy stories about what's happened to us in the past, both on and off the pitch. Less and I have known each other for such a long time – we've basically grown up together – that we've got endless stories to tell.

We even get to invite special guests! On one episode, Mary Earps stood in for Vick and asked the questions. On another episode, we dragged Leah Williamson along to chat. We even filmed one episode in Ibiza – that was UNREAL.

The Tooney & Russo Show works like a dream. Usually. Because she plays for Arsenal (forward, jersey number 23), Less already lives down south, so I travel down there to record at the studio in London. We film a couple of episodes in the evening, and then go out for a meal. The next morning, we get up early and film a couple more. So in the space of 24 hours, we cram in four episodes, a meal out and bonus chatting time. Or at least, that's the plan.

Poor Less . . . last night, even though we both had a hotel room each, we decided to have a sleepover in the same one, so we could catch up properly. But pretty much instantly, it turned into the worst sleepover ever because Less started throwing up. And carried on throwing up. And then threw up some more. And maybe a bit more after that. She was REALLY ill. This morning, there was no way she could film *anything*, so in the end I just made sure she was OK, hugged her goodbye and went back to Manchester.

So the podcast is USUALLY a nice reason to get together. But, on balance, it's even nicer when one of us doesn't have her head down the loo.

AN UNFORGETTABLE NIGHT

Yep. Still on the train. I know what I'll do. I'll write about a night that wasn't just awesome. It wasn't even doubly awesome. IT WAS TRIPLY AWESOME.

ELLA TOONE

I remember 26 October 2021 like it was just yesterday. The Lionesses were playing against Latvia in a World Cup qualifier in Riga, and we were just eight minutes in . . .

Lauren Hemp crossed the ball towards the goal. The Latvian defenders attempted to clear it, but then the ball was right there in front of me, just waiting for me to score.

So I did!

I PUT THE BALL IN THE BACK OF THE NET and scored the first goal of the match.

But that was just the start, because four minutes later, Fran Kirby took Beth Mead's ball and nudged it in my direction. I went for it AND SCORED . . . AGAIN!

Everyone started saying that I was going to get a hat trick*. But you don't think of that when you're on the pitch. You just want to play your best game and help contribute to the team's performance . . . and the team was going for it!

Ellen White scored. Then Millie Bright. By half time, the score was Latvia 0 – England 4. Pretty good, right? Ha. Well, we weren't done yet! In the second half, Beth Mead scored to make it 0 – 5. And then, in the sixty-eighth minute I got the

---

* A hat trick is when a footballer scores three goals in the same match. But can you believe that the term has zero to do with magic? Instead, it comes from the cricket pitch. If a bowler took three wickets on the trot (meaning that they bowled out or otherwise got rid of three members of the other team using just three balls, one after another), they were given a hat by the club in recognition of this impressive achievement. So because the prize was a hat and maybe because bowling out three players – bish, bash, bosh – was a neat trick, they called it a HAT TRICK.

ball. I fell, I got up and I took a shot. The Latvian goalie tried to deflect it, but . . . GOOOOOOOOAL!

A hat trick is a big deal when you're playing for any team. Scoring three goals in one match? Yes, PLEASE. But when it's a hat trick for England, it's so far out of this world, it's somewhere past Jupiter. And the game wasn't over yet.

Rachel Daly knocked in another goal two minutes later, before Leah Williamson banged in one more. Then, almost immediately afterwards, Georgia Stanway took her turn. And Daly finished off the match with her second goal and England's tenth to make the final score Latvia 0 – England 10.

This wasn't just a great match for me; it was a total team triumph.

ONE IN A MILLION

I'm finally back home! And OMG. My mum is THE BEST.

When I left, the house was an absolute tip. The bedroom looked as if a minor tornado had blown through it. The dirty dishes were all piled up. My training kit was NEAR the washing machine, but not actually IN it. There were so many things at the bottom of the stairs, waiting to go up, that there could have been a small animal living inside the heap and I wouldn't have known. And I'm pretty sure there was a dirty sock hanging off one of the lampshades.

The thing is, if you play for Manchester United AND you're on the England squad, life is already stupidly busy. Although I've also got to admit that there's another factor here: cleaning and tidying are NOT my superpowers. Even if I weren't a footballer, if there were an Olympic medal for cooking and cleaning, I would NOT win it. I'm not even sure I'd come in the top eight billion.

I'm so awful at the whole housework thing, in fact, that my mum still insists on doing it for me. She comes round once a week to sort it all out. And she's clearly been round today (THANK GOODNESS) because now it's SPOTLESS!

My mum's a big fan of houses that are so totally immaculate and germ-free that you could do an actual medical operation on the kitchen worktop. So just in case a surgeon is reading this and finds themselves suddenly looking for a spare room where they can yank out an appendix or a pair of tonsils, I'll let you know when Mum's been round and you can pop over!

Anyway, she won't take no for an answer. And she lives just four minutes away, so at least it's not far, but still. She really is one in a million.

P.S. PHEW!

I thought for a minute that Mum had accidentally got rid of my ridiculously big candle collection when she was cleaning, but she hadn't. All thirty-four candles are safe!

I'm totally not joking. That's how many I've got in the drawer right now. I'm EXCELLENT at hoarding candles (and diffusers – I love those too). My mum's always going on about them, saying, 'Ella, you need to burn these!'

But I never want to! I can't bring myself to light them and watch them burn away, even if I know they're going to smell out of this world when I do.

Tell you what, though – the inside of my drawer smells AMAZING.

SHE SHOOTS . . . SHE SCORES!

We had a *sick* shooting practice today. It was like the net was magnetic – the balls just kept going in, one after another. I was BUZZING.

THE NOT-SO-SECRET DIARY OF A FOOTBALLER

I always have a shooting session at the end of training. Some players might join in with me. Some players do it some days and not others. But as a midfielder, I always need to be ready to fire one in the net, so I practise A LOT.*

When I'm shooting, I always like to have a goalkeeper in the net because then it's like a real game. When there's no keeper between me and the goal, there's a danger of overthinking where to put the ball. I miss a lot more when

---

* Look! It's a footnote about a foot! I'm right-footed. That doesn't mean I can't kick a ball with my left foot, just that I *prefer* using my right. If I'm going to score a goal, I'm able to boot it harder with my right foot too. You might be right-footed OR left-footed. Some players are both-footed, which means they can control the ball equally well with both their left and right foot. If you're not sure which is your preferred foot, try kicking a ball. You'll soon find out!

there's no keeper. I know, right? WEIRD, but 100 per cent true.

I think shooting's like a box of chocolates. You wouldn't pick the same type of chocolate over and over again – you'd be like, 'NO MORE STRAWBERRY DELIGHTS.' It's important to mix it up a bit with, say, purple ones or green triangles. So here are a few of the ~~chocolates~~ shots I go for:

- Shots with the left foot

- Shots with the right foot

- Shots from outside the box

- Shots from crosses

- ⚽ Reaction shots

- ⚽ Replay shots*

WORK? NEVER!

This morning I went to buy something from the shops, and the person at the till recognized me and asked me if I was off to work later. I *do* have training later but my automatic reply was, 'Er . . . no?'

Yes, I put on a kit and go to a training ground, and I play football. But to me, that doesn't feel like going to work.

---

* Let me explain what I mean by this. If I've missed a shot in a game, I'll go over it in training the following week. Then I'll practise the same shot over and over again. That way, I'll know how to put it away better next time.

The truth is, I do work hard. But I love it. And I know how lucky I am to play football. So while it might not feel like work, it actually is . . .

THE BEST JOB IN THE WORLD.

BULLSEYE!

Time for a quiet night in. You might think that this is the ideal opportunity to sprawl on the sofa and binge a Netflix series . . . but I probably won't, for the simple reason that I'm absolutely rubbish at sitting still. Pretty much the SECOND I sit down to watch something on TV, I switch it off to go and do something else.

Thinking about it, this might be part of the reason why I move around the pitch so much. I'm always here, there and everywhere. Always looking for chances that might turn into goals. Always ready to receive the ball and thump it into the net. Always ready to attack, and never standing still.

When I have nights off, I'll usually go and see my mum and spend some time with her. A lot of my friends have babies now too, so sometimes I'll pop in and visit them.

But – BREAKING NEWS – my nights in have changed recently because of my brand-new hobby. And it might *not* be what you expect.

Are you ready?

I've become obsessed with . . . **DARTS**.

ELLA TOONE

You might think that sounds weird. I mean, darts and football feel like they're WORLDS apart. But seriously, don't write it off. Darts is SO GOOD.

I've got all the kit (not that you actually need much). I have a dartboard in my living room and my own darts, and I'm constantly playing it. And the amazing thing is that I don't get bored of it! So if you want to know the formula for a great evening, as far as I'm concerned, it's . . .

PLAY SOME DARTS + EAT NICE FOOD = THE PERFECT CHILLED NIGHT IN

P.S. If I absolutely HAVE to sit still and watch a film, it's got to be *Legend* (2015). It's about London gangsters the Kray twins, and it stars Tom Hardy AS BOTH TWINS. I love it, though at two hours, twelve minutes long, it is the ULTIMATE sitting-still challenge – and there's NO WAY ON EARTH I'm going to sit through the credits too.

STOP PRESS!

All this talk of darts reminds me about my other new favourite game: dominoes! At England camp, the other Lionesses and I love playing games together after training. So this time around I'm going to take dominoes with me for us to play together.

I'm ALWAYS playing dominoes at the moment. My mum's a fan too. It's a dead chill game and I think the girls will love it. I've been telling them

ALL about it. So I'll have to teach them that and see if it knocks Partners* off the number-one spot.

RAIN, RAIN, RAIN

No prizes for guessing what the weather's doing today!

England has a pretty solid reputation for rain. But Manchester *especially* is known for its rain.** I mean, it's obviously raining today. It rained yesterday. The chances are, it'll rain tomorrow and maybe even the day after. And that's OK – I'd far rather play in a massive downpour than I would in

---

* More about this later!
** On average, it rains in Manchester 152 days a year. The average rainfall there is 86.71 cm a year, which is more than half my height!

the blazing sun. I seem to play better when I'm soaked through.

Remember the England match that I wrote about earlier, when I got the hat trick and we thrashed Latvia . . .? It was one of the Lionesses' best games ever, and I do wonder sometimes if our performance had just a little bit to do with the biblical rain pouring down over Daugava Stadium in Latvia. It absolutely bucketed down. I can also confirm that it was absolutely FREEZING. Exactly like Manchester, in fact.

So maybe that's why we got on so well there – it felt JUST like home. ♥

ELLA TOONE

THREE LION(ESSE)S ON A SHIRT

It was the BIG REVEAL for the new England kit today! And . . . I LOVE IT. The traditional three lions – though if you squint a bit, I'm pretty sure you'll agree that they're actually lionesses – are on the left (if you're wearing the kit, that is). My number's on the front and the back, obvs, as out on the pitch, we NEED to know who's who. My name's on the back too, so commentators and fans can easily recognize me. (Not because I need to be reminded of my own name when I put it on.)

Anyway, it fit PERFECTLY. And that's when the nerves kicked in. It's only a few days now until we set off for the England camp ahead of the actual tournament, so we don't have long to get everything right. We need to be at peak fitness. We need to perfect our set pieces. All the usual stuff, really. But we've done it before, and I'm feeling confident we can do it again!

IT HAPPENED ON A DOG WALK

I've just got back from walking my dog, Norman, and I'm DRENCHED. It's another rainy day up north. Otherwise, it was a pretty uneventful walk: he weed on six lampposts, he sniffed at least 274 dogs' bottoms, he barked at me in the park until I gave him a treat, I picked up his poo, and we came home. Like I said, apart from getting soaking wet, it was nothing special.

It was certainly NOTHING like the dog walk I went

on in September 2020 that changed my life for ever. It was during that dog walk when Phil Neville – who was the England manager from 2018 until 2021 – rang me to say that he was calling me up to the next England camp. I had NO idea what to say. I'm pretty sure I thanked him (or at least I hope I did – my mum will be cross if I didn't). And he told me that he thought I really deserved it.

YAAAAAAAAAAAAAAAAAAAAAYYYYYYYYY!

OMG I was buzzing. And as soon as I put the phone down, I rang my mum and dad and they were buzzing too!

That memory still instantly has me covered in goosebumps. (Just to clarify, that's goosebumps from remembering the sheer thrill of it, of course. I'm a Northerner. We don't get cold.)

THE NOT-SO-SECRET DIARY OF A FOOTBALLER

Playing for England is something that I'd dreamed of ever since I was a little girl, while I was making my way slowly, slowly through the age groups: the under-17s, under-19s, under-21s . . . It was always my dream to play for the England seniors one day. I tried to imagine what it would feel like running out on to the pitch, wearing the fabled England shirt and representing my country. I wished for it so hard that sometimes I thought I might burst.

Then it actually happened.

(I was called up, I mean. I didn't burst.)

I remember being so nervous when I got to the camp for the first time. There were a lot of Manchester City girls there that I'd met back when I was with the team, so that made it a

ELLA TOONE

bit easier. But I was still very anxious. I was worried that I wasn't good enough. I was training with the best players in England, and I was one of the youngest. For a while, I wondered why I'd even been selected. It took some time for me to get into the flow of training because it was pretty intense, but once I got my head around it and settled in, being there was AWESOME.

What I didn't realize though is that you don't just get called up to play for England once and then automatically get picked to play every time. Each time there's a new camp, the players are carefully selected and then called up all over again, because the manager wants the best players RIGHT AT THAT MOMENT. You can't ever take an England call-up for granted because you can't guarantee that you'll be selected again.

So that means that before every England camp, you're waiting . . . waiting . . . waiting to see if you'll be going back this time. It's nerve-wracking. But once the call comes, you're on cloud nine.

It's one of the best feelings EVER.

GOOOOOOOOOOOOOOOAL!

Sorry! I can't resist reliving my first England match – you don't mind, right? It was pretty special . . .

On 23 February 2021 – when I was 21 – I made my senior international debut for England in a friendly against Northern Ireland. I came on at half time and we won, 6-0!

But see those six goals? That's the best bit. One of those goals was actually MINE. I took a penalty . . . and scored!

Back. Of. The. Net.

A SNEAK PREVIEW!

Now that I've started thinking back to when I became a Lioness, I CAN'T STOP THINKING ABOUT BEING A LIONESS. And with our next tournament round the corner – if you'll excuse even more capital letters – I CAN'T STOP THINKING ABOUT THE ENGLAND CAMP, EITHER.

I'm in the very privileged position of knowing what

THE NOT-SO-SECRET DIARY OF A FOOTBALLER

an England training camp is actually like, so I'm going to interrupt my not-so-secret diary yet again with some insider knowledge. That way, if you ever go to an England camp, you'll know what to expect.

Unsurprisingly, England training is quite similar to the training at Manchester United.

1. Wake up!

2. Go to the physio room and fill in a form about how I'm feeling and my general well-being. This includes questions about how well I've slept and how my body feels. We all have to do this every single day, just so the team can keep track of how we're doing.

ELLA TOONE

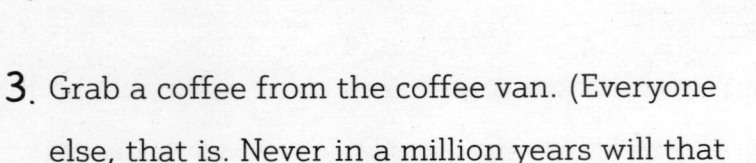

3. Grab a coffee from the coffee van. (Everyone else, that is. Never in a million years will that be me. Ewww.)

4. Have a DELICIOUS breakfast.

5. Go to a team meeting. If anyone ever tells you that football is just a bunch of people kicking a ball about, don't believe a word of it, because it's SO much more than that! In a big tournament, there's loads of analysis that goes on behind the scenes. We talk about who we're going to play against and how we're going to play. For example, there might be new players on the other team who change the dynamic, and we need to figure out how to deal with their tactics. We talk about training and what we need to work

on to make sure that we're playing our best. And we talk about set pieces that we want to get ready for the next game.

6. Warm up in the gym before training.

7. Train on the pitch for anything between 30 and 90 minutes.

8. Shooting practice! At the England camp, there are always a lot of players who practise shooting after the training session. It works like this: pass it in, set it and then have a shot from outside the box. There are always keepers in the net, and there are always a LOT of players in the queue waiting for their turn to shoot.

9. Back to the gym!

10. Have a DELICIOUS tea. (There's an awful lot of really good food at an England camp.)

And then we have the rest of the day or evening to entertain ourselves, which we tend to do with card games and board games.

I CAN'T WAIT.

ME AND MY LASHES

I'm known for my lashes, which is a bit mad. But for anyone who thinks I was born like this and that these lovely, thick, black, feathery lashes are 100 per cent natural, I've got bad news.

They don't really look like that.

I get them done every three weeks at the lash bar.

(Soz.)

In fact, I've been to get new lash extensions today, so they're as good as new again. Yay!

Seriously though, there's a really good reason why I have extensions. Basically I look really young without them. I'm totally not kidding. Ages ago I started wearing extensions and loved them. And then I tried going without them, but I just didn't look like me. Or rather, I did look like me, but the me from a VERY long time ago.

So back the lashes came!

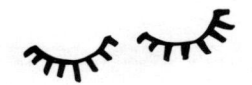

ELLA TOONE

My lashes are pretty special actually. They're called volume lashes, and the lash technician makes them look really long and thick. They're applied by attaching fake lashes to my own teeny tiny lashes, one by one. How clever is that?

They're hard work to keep on top of to be honest, but totally worth it. I always sleep on one side, which means that one eye's lovely, but then when I'm getting near to my next appointment, the other looks like a spider on its last legs.

Not everyone's bothered about lashes and make-up, of course. Some of the players go on to the pitch completely make-up free. But that's what's great about being one of the Lionesses: we're all wearing the same strip, so everyone already knows we're on the same side. What we do with our faces and our hair and, yes, even our lashes is totally up to us.

I AM OFFICIALLY NOT A MORNING PERSON

Some people leap out of bed, stick on a smile and jump straight into a song-and-dance routine when their alarm goes off.

Some don't.

And some REALLY don't. (I'm one of *these* people.)

Let's take this morning's alarm, for example. (Can someone PLEASE take my alarm clock and drop it down a well or something??) Anyway, the alarm went off at 5.30 a.m., a time that shouldn't even be allowed. But because I'm off to a make-up shoot* in London, which is about 200 miles away, it means catching a train practically the day before.

In my defence, I sleep like a baby. I need a LOT of sleep – probably because of all the exercise I get when I'm awake. So if I haven't had enough ZZZZZs, then I'm horrible with a capital H. People don't chat to me in the morning for a reason. The good news is that I'm a lot better than I used to be – just ask my mum. The bad news is that before 9 a.m., I absolutely, completely, 100 per cent cannot talk to anyone.

---

* Let's just get one thing straight: at any reasonable time of the day, make-up shoots are totally THE most glamorous thing ever and I love, love, LOVE them. It's the getting out of bed at half past ridiculous o'clock that I'm allergic to. That and grass.

Fun fact! Less reckons she's such a champion sleeper that she could fall asleep on a camel's back. As someone who's spent a lot of time hammering on Alessia Russo's hotel room door, trying to wake her up after she's accidentally knocked her alarm off, I'm prepared to agree. But I'd also like to see her sleeping on a camel, because that would be some serious sleep gymnastics.

BEING AN ACTUAL CELEB

It's OK, you can relax. I didn't miss the photo shoot! I'm here right now and it's after 9 a.m., which means I'm considerably less of an ogre and wayyyyyy more human.

ELLA TOONE

So, seeing as I'm sitting in a fancy hotel suite being treated like royalty, I thought I'd write a bit about stardom. You know, being famous and all that. I'm still not quite sure how it's happened, but I seem to have accidentally become an actual celeb, which is officially NUTS.

Just so you don't think I'm a total princess though, a fair chunk of my life IS exceedingly normal. I don't live in a palace with servants, and eat croissants dusted with actual gold for breakfast, or have a telly in the bathroom or anything daft like that. But I've got to admit that the star treatment every now and again is INSANELY good. I spend most of my time in a tracksuit or a football kit, so I love getting styled and dressed up for a change.

Honestly, today's shoot has been like something out of a film. I've had a whole team of people fussing around me. They came armed with suitcases FULL of make-up and made me look A-MA-ZING. (They even fixed my missing lashes, which desperately needed redoing.)

There are so many clothes that it feels like a shop in here. Except it's not like on the high street, where you're hunting through the racks for the right size. This is a shop just for me because . . . EVERYTHING fits. They've ONLY brought me clothes in my exact size. *Mind. Blown.* I didn't go for anything really bizarre though, because then I wouldn't feel – or look – like myself. Instead, I picked a classy suit that's – well, NICE. (The price tag isn't, though. My nan would be horrified.)

ELLA TOONE

SO FAR PAST BEDTIME, IT'S NEARLY ALARM O'CLOCK AGAIN

It's all over now, but WOW. What an epic day.

Once I was ready – made up, hair done, suited, booted and dripping with borrowed jewellery – I was whisked away to The Prince's Trust event at a theatre in London called the Theatre Royal Drury Lane, and I walked up AN ACTUAL RED CARPET. I was interviewed by the press. I had my photo taken. SOMEONE HELD AN UMBRELLA OVER MY HEAD. To top it all off, the event was awesome AND inspiring. I did so much clapping, I was in serious danger of turning into a seal.

THE NOT-SO-SECRET DIARY OF A FOOTBALLER

I've been to a few of these sort of events now, and I've loved every single one. Another of my absolute faves was the Pride of Britain Awards, which celebrate the nation's unsung heroes. You know, people who do awesome stuff but never make the headlines? It gave me such a warm glow just to be in the same room as so many amazing winners. I wore this gorgeous royal-blue dress with spaghetti straps. It had a drapey neckline and a wide belt and – get this! – my boyfriend's tie matched the dress!

That was the night that the Lionesses won the Inspiration Award. Rather than get all awkward explaining it, I'll simply tell you what the Pride of Britain Awards' people said:

THE LIONESSES England's European Champions did more than win a trophy – they galvanized the nation and gave a whole generation new role models.

Pretty cool, eh? Anyway, we were all invited on to the stage to receive the award, and I felt SO proud to be up there with all of my mates. (It was very nice winning too, if I'm honest.)

And then there was the time the Lionesses won the 2022 BBC Sports Personality Team of the Year after we won the Euros. (That evening, I had my hair in an up-do and wore an awesome mulberry halter-neck dress. I felt a million dollars!) Everyone was so emotional to have won, and it was an INCREDIBLE evening.

Do you know what? I might whinge about mornings, but every one of these events was more than worth getting up for.

(I'm quite pleased I have a lie-in tomorrow though.)

ALARM O'CLOCK

I just switched off my morning alarm clock and have picked up my diary and pen straight away – I'm sort of getting into this writing thing!

Hey, you might be thinking, why isn't Tooney ranting about how much she hates alarm clocks? Isn't this the part where she petitions the UK Government for them all to be dropped into an active volcano?

A-ha. That's because my alarm's on my phone, so there's no way I'm dunking that in lava. But also because my alarm today wasn't set for ridiculous o'clock – it was set for the semi-respectable hour of 10 a.m.

ELLA TOONE

Bliss. ♡

I used to think that unless I stayed in bed until midday, it wasn't technically a lie-in. But I've got a day off, and now that I've reached my grand old age, I don't want to waste the day. So that's why I set the alarm. Ten minutes later, I'm out of the house! No messing.

When it's my day off, there's usually stuff I need to get done. Sometimes I have errands to run. Maybe I'll have a clear out of all the rubbish in my house that I don't use any more. And believe it or not, just like my eyelashes, my nails don't look this fabulous on their own either, so I might have to squeeze in an essential visit to the beauty salon too. If I get the chance to meet up with Less, we'll do a bit of shopping and there's always – ALWAYS – food. (Chicken katsu curry, but with amai sauce instead of katsu sauce, just FYI. We both have EXACTLY the same because it's SO delicious.)

A WEIRD WEEKEND

It's Monday!!! Whoop!!! Here's a shocker for you: I like Mondays. For most people, the weekend is Saturday and Sunday, right? Well, it's different for footballers. In the Women's Super League, match day is usually Sunday, making it THE busiest day of the week. There's no way we can take Saturday or Sunday off, so we usually have a Monday and a Thursday off instead.

Here's what a typical week in my life looks like when I'm NOT getting ready for a tournament. In the build-up to a tournament, matches can be any day of the week, so our timetable is TOTALLY up in the air.

Monday (that's today!)

A day off! A Monday that feels like a Sunday (we can call it Smonday, if you like) is SURPRISINGLY fun. I'll often pop round to my friends' houses and play with their babies. I'll also get some food and go shopping. All the shops are quiet, so it's the PERFECT time.

Tuesday

It's time to get back to training. Yay! I start to get twitchy when I don't play. Plus, if we rest for too long, we'll lose our form. So I can't wait to get back to the drills and exercises that maintain our stamina and keep us fighting fit. Today it's just a single session, which means we'll be on the pitch.

Wednesday

Wednesday is very much like Tuesday, but it's that bit closer to our next match day, so we're revving up for the game. After the training session on the pitch, we'll have a gym session too. We'll also spend some time taking a closer look at the opposing team, studying their form, working out our tactics and making a plan for the match.

Thursday

Time for another day off! BOOM. It's officially the second half of our weekend! I love a Thursday. It's the perfect day of the week to take a load off and relax before everything (ALERT: HORRIBLY PREDICTABLE FOOTBALL PHRASE INCOMING!) kicks off again. (Sorry.)

Friday

We're back to training! WHOOP! Like Wednesday, we have a gym session after training on the pitch. Things are properly hotting up!

Saturday

IT'S THE DAY BEFORE MATCH DAY. This is when we'll do a short, sharp session to go over the things that we've worked on during the week. If we've got an away game tomorrow, we'll travel down after training on Saturday and stay over in a hotel.

Sunday

IT'S FINALLY MATCH DAY!

After the game, it's time for a debriefing. We pick the match to pieces, bit by bit, working out what went well (and what definitely didn't). Any injuries are assessed and treatment plans sorted out. It's pretty full on. And then everything starts all over again!

My weekend isn't *always* Monday and Thursday. Schedules change, especially if we're building up to a tournament, so it can be a bit random. But we get a fair bit of notice, which means we can plan what we want to do on our days off.

So there it is. Unless you're a footballer yourself, my split weekend might seem a bit on the weird side, but if you're THINKING of becoming a footballer (EXCELLENT idea, by the way),

ELLA TOONE

I can reliably inform you that it can actually be really fun!

THE DAY WE HID GEORGIA STANWAY IN A SUITCASE*

I can't believe it. After what feels like WEEKS of counting down the days to the England camp, WE'RE GOING TOMORROW. Despite being not-so-secretly worried about the tournament, now that it's nearly here, I'm suddenly so excited that I could do a conga round Tyldesley town centre RIGHT NOW.

---

* Yes, you read that right.

THE NOT-SO-SECRET DIARY OF A FOOTBALLER

Things I am most excited about

- ⚽ Being reunited with Less

- ⚽ Meeting the newbies

- ⚽ Hanging out with EVERYONE

- ⚽ Singing (badly and VERY LOUDLY) on the coach

- ⚽ Arguing over who gets the best room (though everyone already knows it'll be Mary Earps – she always works some magic and ends up with a room big enough for the entire England squad)

- ⚽ THE FOOD

- The pranks

- Having a laugh with my best mates

- ALL THE FOOTBALL

Things I am nervous about

- Missing my boyfriend and my dog

- Reassuring the manager that picking me for the squad WAS the right decision

- Packing (something else I'm allergic to)

Anyway, to celebrate being one day away from our departure date – and also because I actually need something to put all my stuff in – I've finally dragged the suitcase out of the loft.

THE NOT-SO-SECRET DIARY OF A FOOTBALLER

I've got two problems with suitcases:

1. I have absolutely zero idea of what to put in them (apart from pants).

2. They ALWAYS give me the giggles.

I can't even LOOK at a suitcase any more without laughing, as they remind me of a HILARIOUS afternoon at a different training camp, way back in 2017.

Less and I were in Jordan at the Under-17s Women's World Cup. We were meant to be studying, but we were actually trying not to fall asleep because it was SO dull. We were desperate to find a way to liven things up. So we idly wondered if we could fit Georgia Stanway into a suitcase. Except, because we were supposed to be studying, we thought we'd better make it a tiny bit educational. (If you'd been there, I can absolutely guarantee that you would've done it too.)

LUGGAGE-BASED EXPERIMENT

Prediction: We predict that Georgia Stanway will fit into my suitcase.

Evidence: Georgia Stanway is only 1.62 metres tall, so when she scrunches herself up a bit, she's practically suitcase-sized.

Equipment: Georgia Stanway and a suitcase.

Method: Squeeze Georgia Stanway into the suitcase and drag her around a bit, like actual luggage.

Results: IT WORKED. And the suitcase had four wheels, so it was a v-e-r-y smooth ride for Georgia. She was laughing just as much as we were when we unzipped her.

WARNING: Please do not try this at home (or, in fact, anywhere else). Now that I'm a bit older and wiser, I know that it was actually quite a dangerous thing to do. Oops.

THE DREADED PACKING

It's been six hours since I took the suitcase out. I can't avoid the packing any longer.

Except if I write a bit more in this diary, I sort of can . . .

ELLA TOONE

I could tell you, for instance, how packing is right up there with jet lag as one of my least favourite things in the world. It shouldn't be – I've done it so many times now that I should be excellent at putting things in a suitcase. (Because that's all it is, isn't it? We're not talking about actual rocket science.) But I'm SO bad at it. I'm mega disorganized. I can never look ahead and imagine what I'll need, so I can never decide what to pack. And I worry about forgetting things, so I leave it until the last possible minute (which is RIGHT NOW, clearly). And then I faff (which is why you're enjoying a bonus diary entry).

I know. I'll do this a different way, by making a list of what I need:

THE NOT-SO-SECRET DIARY OF A FOOTBALLER

- *Earbuds – something I NEVER forget*

- *Sliders – I need these to wear in the shower (I can't stand it when people don't)*

- *Hairspray – REALLY important*

- *Lip balm – totally essential*

- *A book to read – I love a football autobiography, me*

- *Colouring books and pens – for when we're chilling, and I just want to switch off my mind and relax*

- *Word searches – really cool for downtime too*

- *A portable speaker – to blast music in the room and get me in the mood for a match*

- *Eyelash brushes – I take at least three of these as they have a dreadful habit of vanishing*

- *Trainers – I've treated myself to a brand-new white pair. They won't stay that colour for long, but right now, they are SICK*

Actually, there ARE two things that I know I will always remember to pack now. So even if I forget everything else, I know I'll have these:

- *My red hat – after losing my dad, this is my number-one most important thing to pack. We got this from the hospital, and I take it on trips, to games and to training. It goes everywhere with me*

- *My special sports bra – this has a heart sewn into it for Dad, and I wear it for every match*

WHEN I WORE A BUCKET HAT FOR THREE DAYS STRAIGHT

ALERT: This is obviously even more packing avoidance. Maybe if I keep thinking of things to write about, I'll NEVER have to pack and my mum will come round and help me like the olden days . . .?!*

If we're going to a hot place, like, say, Australia, I make sure to take a couple of bucket hats with me. I love them. They're my perfect multi-purpose hat. First up, they keep the sun off my face REALLY well. Second, they look good. The third reason is

---

* She didn't. Argh!!

that after we won the Euros in 2022, I wore a red England bucket hat for about three days solid, so they make me think of WINNING, which is a good thing if you're heading off to a tournament!

Don't tell anyone, but there's a secret, fourth reason for the non-stop-bucket-hat-wearing after the Euros. That's because my hair was a genuine MESS. After we won the Euros (I haven't banged on about this nearly enough yet, so I'm just putting it out there again), we didn't have a moment to ourselves. It was all parties, interviews, TV appearances and photo shoots. Lionesses this; Lionesses that. Did I have time to do my hair? No, I did not. But the red bucket hat that I wore after we won (WE WON!!!) was the perfect way to disguise the fact that my hair looked untidier than my bedroom floor. So I put it on my head and left it there.

The bad news: I lost that beautiful bucket hat.

The good news: I know where to get another one if I need it!

There is a pub in Tyldesley that has a mural of me on the side. (If you've never been, it's worth a visit. Their pies, chips and gravy are SO good. And did I mention that they have a WHOLE MURAL OF ME ON THE SIDE?! Ah, I did. Well, some things are so good, you have to say them twice.)

The last time I went, they were selling – well, BUCKETS of bucket hats, plastered with the words **BUZZIN' MI HEAD OFF**. Apparently I said this quite a lot after the Euros (which we won! Did I mention that?), and I'll have to take their word for it. It's all a bit of a blur, but it sounds like the sort of thing I'd come out with, so I'm guessing it's true!

FOOTBALL'S GETTING REAL!

Even though the tournament doesn't start for two weeks, this is usually when the Lioness machinery whirrs into action. There are loads of reasons we set off early:

1. Leaving real life behind allows us to FOCUS on the task ahead.

2. We have a chance to BOND as a team.

3. There's oodles of time for extra TRAINING.

4. There's TIME TO BREATHE when we arrive, and no last-minute panicking.

5. We can properly SETTLE IN to our surroundings.

I wonder if I'll be able to sleep . . .*

MY ALL-TIME FAVOURITE KARAOKE SONG

I can SEE the tour bus! I can't wait to get on board! Pretty soon, I'm going to start singing, and then everyone else will be desperate for us to get there so the noise will stop.

---

* Don't worry. I totally slept. Not even a brass band playing 'Football's Coming Home' could keep me awake at night.

ELLA TOONE

Fun fact! I LOVE SINGING.

If, at this point, you're imagining me in some sort of cartoony woodland scene, sitting on a log and charming the birds out of the trees with the voice of an angel (like that bit in *Sleeping Beauty*), then I'm going to have to burst your bubble. Because I have a TERRIBLE voice. And I'm not being modest here – ask anyone who knows me and they'll tell you that it's really, really bad.

Does that stop me?

Nah!

Even though my voice is dodgy enough to make dogs howl (on a good day, maybe it could even shatter a window), I still sing all the time. I sing in the changing rooms, I sing in the shower, and I sing on the pitch. I even used to have this special tune that I sang first thing in the morning on a match day, until I decided that I was being way, way too superstitious. Did I REALLY think that singing a daft song would somehow futureproof the game? Err, no. Was the result far more likely to be about our fitness and skill? Err, yeah. So I stopped and gave everyone's eardrums a break.

There's one song that I love more than any other in the entire world. I'm not sure you'll know it because it's dead old (it was written in 1983!), though your parents might. And it's a country-and-western song. In fact, I bet you'd never guess it in a million years, so I'm going to put you out of your misery. My favourite song of all time is called . . . 'Islands in the Stream'.

ELLA TOONE

If right now you're scratching your head and looking as if someone's just asked you the best way to split the atom, let me give you a little more detail. 'Islands in the Stream' is a song by the Bee Gees, recorded by legendary country singers Dolly Parton and Kenny Rogers, and it's an absolute BANGER. It's also an awesome one to sing along to. So whenever there's even a glimpse of a karaoke machine, I'm at the front of the queue. And, get this . . . when I perform it, I pretend to be two people and I SING BOTH PARTS. I'm Dolly AND Kenny.*

Which means that, basically, I don't shut up for the ENTIRE song.

---

* Go on, you know you want to have a listen. I'll just do keepy-uppies for a few minutes so you can look it up on YouTube (or ask a parent or grown-up to play it for you). But I'll tell you something for free: when you get to the chorus for the second time, I'd bet Ronaldo's next pay cheque that you're singing along.

P.S. My back-up tune is 'The Man Who Can't Be Moved' by The Script. That goes down well too. (The song, I mean. Not my voice.)

THE RULES

Before I head off to camp, it's probably worth a little reminder of . . . The Rules.

How scary does that sound? And I'm not even talking actual football rules here. These are the rules for training camp, which are, not-so-coincidentally, pretty much the same rules that we have for matches:

1. Rest MEANS rest. If we're meant to be resting, we should quite literally be putting our feet up. So anything remotely active is banned. No

taekwondo. No rounders. No breakdancing. (You get the gist.)

2. We've absolutely got to wear shin-pads in training, which is totally fine by me. I've always been quite attached to my shins – I'd rather someone else's studs weren't attached to them too.

3. There's absolutely no jewellery allowed under any circumstances. Not even a small stud.

None of these rules is a problem, though. They're not being killjoys; it's just to get us into the right mindset. Basically if you wouldn't do something on a game day, you're not doing it at camp either.

Which is fair enough. I'm happy to follow those rules and get INTO THE ZONE.

I LOVE TRAINING CAMPS ♡

We're here!!

Being here at training camp – living and breathing football – has reminded me what I love about the whole experience.

EVERYTHING.

First off, we go to such cool places. St George's Park in Staffordshire in the UK is the home of all of the FA's (or Football Association's) football teams, including the Lionesses. There are fourteen outdoor pitches – one of them with EXACTLY THE SAME TYPE OF GRASS as Wembley – and a hotel. But we've also trained in the Netherlands, Spain and

Australia. And then we're playing football every single day . . . with the best footballers in the country.

But the real pinch-me bit is training with your best mates. Some of them you might see all the time. Others you don't see a lot. It's a chance to catch up, and it's so much fun.

So, yeah. The training camps are unreal. I'll NEVER get bored of them.

BEST FRIENDS

The thing about football is that you make friends for life when you're very young.

Sooooo many of the Lionesses are my best friends. There's Less, of course. But I'm really good mates with Millie Turner too. I've known Millie for years. Get this, right? We joined Manchester United ON THE SAME DAY (1 July 2018, to be precise), and then we made our debuts in the EXACT SAME MATCH on 19 August 2018. We've been on the Manchester United squad together ever since, and we're really close. Millie is someone who lights up every room that she goes into – she's SO FUN to be around. So it's amazing that she's a Lioness too.

I'm also REALLY lucky to be in the Lioness squad with a load more girls who I grew up with, like Georgia Stanway, Lotte Wubben-Moy and Niamh Charles. A few of us in the team went through all the age groups together as we worked our way up to the senior team, so it makes it even more special that we're still playing together.

ELLA TOONE

And I'm not the only one who's grown up with other Lionesses. Leah Williamson and Keira Walsh have known each other since they were twelve and went to the same training camps. Leah says that she saw how good a player Keira was and stuck to her like glue. She really rates Keira's opinion and so do I. If Keira says you're a good player, that means the world. On the other hand, if her opinion is something that she knows you won't want to hear, she won't say anything as she won't want to upset you. But if Keira does give you a compliment, then you KNOW she means it.

A player who I didn't meet until I was a little older is Mary Earps. We actually clashed at first – we both have strong personalities – but now we've really bonded. Mary says it's because I was born in the same year as her little sister, so she feels a bit protective of me. And even though we wind each other up, we care about each other too.

What I love most about Mary is the way she knows when she's reached her Lioness limit. (I'd better explain, or that'll sound REALLY weird.) Basically, when we're at camp, we spend a lot of time together. And by a lot, I mean **A LOT**. So after a while we can get a tiny bit fed up of each other . . .

When I've had enough of the rest of the team, I'll just sit quietly with Less because I don't really like being on my own. But Mary's the opposite – she loves her own space. So she'll just bluntly tell us that her battery is empty and walk out of the room. I really like that. No messing. Straight to the point.

ELLA TOONE

To be honest, I don't really have any favourites – these Lionesses are ALL some of my fave people in the world!

INTRODUCING OUR FABULOUS MANAGER

We just had SUCH a great team talk from the England manager to kick off training camp. She truly is the best.

And this not-even-slightly-secret diary would not be complete without bigging up the person who helped to make not only MY dreams come true, but the dreams of AN ENTIRE COUNTRY. (That's England, by the way, in case you were in any doubt.)

In 2022, Sarina Wiegman became the first manager to lead an England football team to victory for 56 years! As far as I'm concerned, she's right up there with the greatest of all time.

Some stats to kick things off!

Name: Sarina Petronella Wiegman (Is that the coolest middle name ever or what?!)

Date of birth: 26 October 1969

Nationality: Dutch

Career: Professional footballer, high-school PE teacher AND trophy-winning manager

First team: Kruikelientjes FC 1971 from 1987 to 1988

ELLA TOONE

First professional team: Ter Leede from 1994 to 2003

International career: Netherlands from 1987 to 2001

Number of caps: 104*

---

* On the off-chance that you're not quite as obsessed with football as me (though I'm pretty sure you will be by the time you finish reading this diary), I just need to make it clear that Sarina doesn't own 104 actual caps. I mean, where would she put them all?! She'd need an entire display cabinet – you know, like the ones where people put ornaments or fancy plates? Nah – in sport, a cap means that someone's represented their country in an international game. So if you have ten caps, you've played ten international games for your country. I've done a bit of research (you're welcome) and the tradition dates back to 1886. And actually, when it first started, England players WERE awarded real, true-life white silk caps decorated with a red rose. So, on the one hand, Sarina's lucky that she doesn't need to splash out on a new cabinet just to display her enormous cap collection, but on the other hand, they do sound VERY cool. I don't want to show off, but I've got a few caps myself now. I am *insanely* proud of them all.

THE NOT-SO-SECRET DIARY OF A FOOTBALLER

Positions played: Central midfielder and defender

First managerial role: Ter Leede from 2006 to 2007

First title: Knight of the Order of Orange-Nassau

First statue: A bronze statue in the garden of the Dutch Football Association

First international managerial role: Netherlands from 2017 to 2021

Second international managerial role: England from 2021 to . . . TBC!

If I had to pick just one word for how I feel about Sarina, it would be this one:

RESPECT.

ELLA TOONE

And I really mean that. All the players have a LOT of respect for our manager. We know how lucky we are to have her, and we know just how brilliant she is.

But ultimately, we also need to remember she's the boss. At the end of the day, she's in charge, and she knows what she's talking about.

Basically, you don't mess with the manager.

THE INSIDE SCOOP ON TRAINING CAMP

Training camp. It sounds tough, doesn't it? And to be fair, it can be really full on. But at the same time, it's a lot of fun. We're doing what we love, right? And it's not ALL training – there's also a lot of downtime, when we need to find stuff to do.

Let's get down to basics. Here's what a pretty typical day looks like at camp. In fact, it's what we did today.

We start in the mornings as we all feel a bit fresher then. And when the training begins, we don't take any prisoners. We train **REALLY HARD**.

Afterwards, we often head to the gym to exercise some more and increase muscle strength.

Then we're pretty free!

In the afternoons, we might have a meeting every now and again, but usually we just chill out and R-E-L-A-X. Everyone's got a different way of taking a break – some people go to their rooms, while others might go for a walk or get a treatment.

We're properly looked after. We have these fancy 'biomechanics assessments'; this is a chance for our physiotherapists to look REALLY closely at our walking and running style (hips, legs, knees, feet . . . you name it, they check it). They make sure that everything's moving properly and that our boots fit perfectly.

We can also take ice baths, which are about as bone-chilling as they sound, though afterwards the buzz and adrenaline you feel is AMAZING. But my favourite is the deep-tissue massage. Our physiotherapists seem to know exactly where there's an issue in our bodies – even if we don't – and they get right in there with a massage and give us special exercises to sort it out.

We all come back together again for meals, which are the best times to chat. We're all sitting round a table, eating, and there's lots of banter. I love it.

Then in the evening, everyone does their own thing again. Some choose to go to their room and play on a PlayStation or watch films, whereas a lot of us will play games together or sit around chatting some more.

So on the one hand, we work hard, but on the other, we get plenty of time to recharge our batteries too, all while being surrounded by our best friends.

Doesn't get much better than that, does it?

ELLA TOONE

TRAINING AT THE ENGLAND CAMP VERSUS TRAINING AT MANCHESTER UNITED

We kicked off with an ACE training sesh today! The set pieces went like clockwork, and the drills were on point. I mean, Mary Earps has a habit of getting in the way of the ball, but that's her job, I suppose. Leah Williamson and Keira Walsh were passing REALLY well. EVERYTHING just seemed to flow. It really feels as if we're playing as a team!

I always enjoy going to training with the England team. When you look at it, training at an England camp is a lot like training at Manchester United. We do the same sort of stuff, and both

England and Manchester United training sessions are really fun. But at the England camps it can feel REALLY competitive. Not in a scary way – it's just that you're training with some of the best players in England and, let's face it, the best players IN THE WORLD. So you always want to play at your absolute best.

The other difference is that at England camps, you're not going home every night; you're all together for ten days or more, with different people who you've not seen for a long time. That's A LOT of time spent together, both on and off the pitch. So the whole thing can feel really intense.

The absolute best bit about training with the Lionesses, though, is being back together on the pitch. Just like when I play for Manchester United, we have the same goal (please excuse the football pun ... I can't help myself!), which is to make sure that we win against the other side, whoever they are!

It's just that with the England team, we're doing it on the world stage.

Gulp.

ELOUISE AND ALYSSA

It was SO funny today. I think I might have even given myself a six-pack from all the belly laughs! Less and I brought our two favourite people back to life! Don't worry – this hasn't suddenly morphed into a hospital drama. But it probably needs a bit of backstory . . .

FULL DISCLOSURE: this is going to sound NUTS. But, hey – what sort of a diary would it be if there weren't the odd embarrassing story in it? So here goes.

You know how it is when you get a bit bored of being YOU? And maybe you might feel like being a completely different person for a change? No? You have no idea what I'm talking about? OK, I did say this was a bit of a nuts story! Well, at one football camp, Less and I decided to change identity. I was bored of being Ella, so I became Elouise instead. And Alessia was Alyssa. On top of that, we were both American and spoke in these completely dodgy accents. (OK, Less's accent wasn't THAT bad. It was pretty good, actually, but then she did live there for three years!)

The really weird thing is that we didn't discuss or plan it at all. We just did it. Suddenly, *ta-daaaaaaaaaa*. We were Elouise and Alyssa. And then, after we'd had this whole conversation as other people, we switched back again. Just like that!

Honestly, it was a right laugh. In fact, it was SO much fun that Elouise and Alyssa made a guest appearance today!

BANANA TRAUMA

I've got a short break between breakfast and the morning training session now, and after witnessing how many bananas there were at breakfast today, I wanted to share some very important BREAKING NEWS:

I can't stand bananas.

Even if I just see a banana sitting innocently in a fruit bowl, it makes me shudder. I don't know if it's the colour (I like to call it dirty yellow – the sort you'd find in a service-station toilet), the icky smell (ewww), the taste (no, just NO) or that weird shape (it just doesn't seem natural to me). Maybe it's the way they go all powdery when they're out of date. No idea. I couldn't even tell you how my banana phobia started. But I can pinpoint the exact moment when it got worse, and that was after the girls at the England camps found out.

They didn't blend them into a smoothie and make

me drink it, or camouflage them in a fruit salad without me realizing, or anything devious like that. It was FAR worse. They hid the world's most despicable fruit IN MY BED.

BANANARRRRRRGHHHHHH!!!

I'm over it now. Mostly. But I learned the hard way that I should never tell a fellow footballer that I have an irrational dislike of a particular fruit. (Or veg, just to be on the safe side. Or let's face it, ANYTHING.) Because I will never live it down.

WORLDS COLLIDING

A funny thing about the England camp is that you're playing *alongside* players who you might have played *against* in a previous match! I've played against quite a few of them this season at Manchester United. But guess what? THIS is a whole lot easier!

It's SO ODD when you come up against your teammates and friends from England in Women's Super League games. The unwritten rule seems to be that before the game, you REALLY don't speak to each other. As soon as you cross the white line, they're not your friends . . . they become your mortal enemies. They're who you want to beat.

Because you've been away at England camps with them and played with them, you know a lot about their game, which sort of gives you an advantage. The thing is, they know a lot about your game too, which immediately cancels that out! So you've just got to do everything you can to make sure you're playing your best and trying to beat them.

As soon as that final whistle blows, that's the time that you actually talk and everything goes back to normal. Like magic, they're your mates again!

But the best thing of all is BEING ON THE SAME SIDE.

Like now.

TUMBLEWEED ALERT

You'd think, wouldn't you, that what with such great mates, the Lionesses' group chat would be

GOING OFF, right? That we'd share funny memes and laugh our socks off at running jokes and make fun of each other and basically have ALL THE FUN?!

Nah.

The group chat is DEAD. And I'm not even joking!

Maybe it's because we're all afraid of posting something and then . . . no one replying. (Can you imagine? THE HORROR!) But the truth is that apart from when you're at camp and the schedule's being put in it, no one breaks the silence.

No one.

THE NUMBER-ONE THING TO DO AT TRAINING CAMP (APART FROM FOOTBALL)

As I've mentioned already, at training camp, we don't JUST train. If we did, everyone would be exhausted, and there'd be injuries all over the place. What we actually do is work hard in the morning and then, in the afternoon and evening, R-E-L-A-X.

I find this a bit of a struggle, to be honest. I'm usually on the go, and I'm not great at pressing pause. But if the manager says we have to give our muscles a break, then that's what we do. So how do we keep ourselves entertained? Well, the answer is usually . . . GAMES.

LOADS of the Lionesses play cards. It's actually a great way to spend time together, and we had an excellent session tonight, lasting a colossal THREE HOURS. It might sound odd, but we NEVER get bored of it, maybe because we mix it up a lot. Whoever wants to play, can play (although I don't like it when there are too many players, because then I don't win as much!). We've got a few different games that we play too, so we don't get sick of the same ones.

If you could do me a favour and imagine a drumroll here (cheers!), I'd like to announce, in reverse order, our favourite card games.

ELLA TOONE

3. TRUMP (for the avoidance of doubt, this is obvs the game, not the president)

Depending on which cards they've been dealt, each player picks a trump suit (spades, diamonds, clubs or hearts), but keeps it secret. Then the game kicks off and we all take turns playing a card following the same suit, if possible. If we can't follow the suit, we play a trump card and . . . I could go on, but it would take sooooooo long to explain that, quite frankly, it would be quicker for you to become a Lioness first and come to an actual training camp to find out in person. (Or ask a favourite auntie to explain. They usually know.) Whatever, it's GREAT.

2. UNO

There are ALWAYS arguments when we play Uno.

Everyone has their own version, and we spend half the time deciding whose rules we're following. Just to give you a little taste, someone (I won't name names) called their version Fruno (don't ask me why) after making up their own dodgy manoeuvres. For example, one of the rules they set is that when a zero is played, all players rotate their cards in the direction of play. And when you play a seven, you choose who to swap hands with, and THEY HAVE TO DO IT. I know, right? Madness.

1. PARTNERS

Personally my favourite way to wind down in the evenings is by playing Partners. This is a game that we play at the England camp that we absolutely BASH. We play it every day. (We'd play it ALL day if we didn't have an actual football tournament to prepare for.)

Partners is a four-player game, so that's usually me and Less versus – maybe – Millie Turner and Maya Le Tissier, although that changes, because loads of the Lionesses LOVE the game. But Less and I are pretty much always partners and overall we are definitely winning* at the game!

The aim of the game is to help your partner to move round the board and get all your counters into the finishing zone. The catch is that you're not really allowed to talk. (As you can probably guess, that makes it REALLY DIFFICULT for me.) It is SO FUN. And it's the perfect game for camp because every game is completely different. It never gets boring! If

---

* Ha! Now it's printed in an actual book, so no one can argue with that!

you're wondering whether to play Partners with your mates, don't wonder: DO IT. I would totally recommend it.

ENGLAND'S NUMBER-ONE PRANKSTER

Arghhh!

Leah Williamson just got me AGAIN. She's got me SO many times. I'd be mad if only I could stop laughing long enough!

Just in case you'd like to scare the living daylights out of one of your friends or siblings too, this is how our esteemed England captain does it:

ELLA TOONE

1. Leah hides. This could be in one of many places – on the other side of a door, or round a corner, or in the dark or . . . seriously, the list is ENDLESS.

2. I appear, not suspecting a thing.

3. Leah bursts out of nowhere and shouts at about a bazillion decibels,

'TOONEY!'

4. I jump out of my skin, drop whatever I'm carrying, occasionally fall over and always yell,

'ARGHHH!'

You'd think I'd learn, right? Maybe I might open a door slowly in case there's someone waiting on the other side to surprise me? Check empty rooms carefully to see if there really is no one in there? Peer round corners? No. Apparently not.

Every. Single. Time.

ROUND THE WORLD*

In training today we had a competition to see who could do the most 'round the worlds'. A 'round the world' is actually my favourite footballing trick. Maybe it's yours too? It's not just an awesome way of developing ball

---

* Just FYI, I flew to Australia with the Lionesses for the World Cup 2023, so I suppose technically I have been *halfway* round the world now – and back again. But my record for actual, non-stop 'round the worlds' is currently SEVEN.

control; it's also a TOP way of impressing your friends. A football coach will tell you how to do it properly, but this is the basic method:

1. Kick a ball in the air with one foot.

2. While the ball is in the air, move your foot round the ball in a complete circle until it's underneath the ball.

3. Kick the ball in the air again.

4. Repeat steps 2 and 3 until either you miss the ball, or the sun goes down and it's too dark to see the actual ball . . . whichever happens first.

FOOD, GLORIOUS FOOD

I need to take a moment to write about the chefs at training camp.

They are SO GOOD.

The chefs tend to do a live station in the morning, where they cook omelettes, pancakes and poached eggs. So we can choose whatever we like, which is awesome. It's like being in a hotel, BUT BETTER. We get to make requests too. Last week, I really fancied a jacket potato with my tea, so I said that and – *ta-daaaaaaa* – jacket potatoes were on the menu. (I've had one every day since, actually. They are absolutely superb.)

The night before a game, Less and I load up on

pasta. (I LOVE fusilli – you know, the twirly ones?) The chef makes a double batch so there's enough for both of us. We have a mixture of tomato sauce and creamy sauce. And there's chorizo, spinach, broccoli, onion and prawns too, which, as far as I'm concerned, makes the PERFECT bowl of pasta.

The chef serves mine up, and THEN goes and ruins it with chilli and sundried tomatoes for Less because she likes 'a bit of a kick'. (YAY! ANOTHER DREADFUL FOOTBALL JOKE!!!)

Whatever – we're both happy. Although not quite as happy as on Sunday, when there's another favourite on the menu . . . ROAST DINNER.

Never mind the football; it's TOTALLY worth going to training camp just for the food.

MY ABSOLUTE FAVOURITE SORT OF BOOK

It's been a full-on day, so I've gone to bed early to read. Anyone who knows me might be quite surprised by this – as you now know, I'm one of those antsy people who can't sit still and struggles to chill. I'm always on the move, so I feel a real sense of achievement when I sit down and read a book. And it's such a good way to switch off.

I'm not into story books – fantasy, thrillers or stuff like that. I prefer an autobiography. But here's the funny bit. I like autobiographies by . . . footballers and football managers.

I know, I know . . . you'd think I'd want a break, wouldn't you? But I'm FASCINATED by their lives.

I've read loads too: Jamie Vardy, Roy Keane, Joe Thompson, Sir Alex Ferguson . . . I just like knowing what they got up to on their way to becoming footballers and managers, about their career paths and what happened to them to make them who they are. I find it SO inspiring.

And maybe that's part of the reason I'm enjoying writing THIS diary. It's a sort of autobiography too, right? And just as I enjoy reading about other footballers and managers and how they've travelled from their grassroots to Wembley and beyond, I'm enjoying writing about what it's been like for me too.

A REALLY SPECIAL BOOK

Another book that I loved is by Sir Chris Hoy. It's

called *All That Matters*, and it's such a good read. It meant a lot to me after losing my dad to prostate cancer. Sir Chris is going through the same thing, and his words have been such a comfort. When I was reading his book, I just switched off from football completely. What a legend.

THIS ONE TIME, AT ENGLAND CAMP

Fun fact! At the beginning of any England camp, we all have a blood test. It's part of the regular medical tests that we need to have to make sure that we're on top form. If I'm honest, it's not my FAVOURITE part of the camp, but hey, it's not a big deal. Except for my VERY FIRST England camp . . .

ELLA TOONE

It was at St George's Park*. I remember going and being ridiculously shy. Luckily I knew a few of the players from Man United and Man City. My great friend Abbie McManus was at the camp as well, so that was a bonus. She really looked after me. We had our blood tests in the morning, and mine was scheduled to be the earliest one. Great – I'd get it over and done with. So I got up really early – so early that it was before breakfast – and went to the physio room to get my blood test done. I remember sitting there, waiting. Katie Zelem was next to me and Leah Williamson was across

---

* Top tip! If you want to sound like you totally know what you're talking about when it comes to football, don't call the home of the England camp by its official name of St George's Park. Call it SGP. You can throw in a knowing nod here to look extra knowledgeable. Just make sure not to call it PSG (Paris Saint-Germain FC) because then your good work will be completely undone and you'll just look a twit.

from me, and they were talking about people who faint when they get bloods done and blah blah blah –

The next thing I remember is WAKING UP ON THE FLOOR.

Argh!!!

I'd fainted at my first England camp, getting my bloods done. IT WAS SO EMBARRASSING.
I remember Zel saying, 'Could somebody get Abbie McManus? She's fainted. She's on the floor.'

So Abbie came in. My really good mate, remember? Well, I looked up at her and she . . . GOT HER PHONE OUT AND STARTED TAKING PICTURES OF ME ON THE FLOOR.

And then, because I'd held the queue up by fainting, when I walked out of the physio room, everyone was sitting in the corridor and they were ALL laughing at me. It was mortifying. I was SO embarrassed.

Now, every time we have bloods taken at the England camp, I always have to be one of the last in the queue. This gives me time to eat beforehand, so I don't faint again.

MY FEET ARE OFFICIALLY FAMOUS

I know that sounds nuts – I couldn't believe it either. I've just been having some downtime after training and discovered that my feet have their own website. REALLY. It's just photos of me and my feet. Loads of photos. It's literally the daftest thing I've ever seen.

In most of the photos, you can see my toes, which I'm not totally thrilled about because they're my least favourite extremities. I'm not keen on the rest of my feet either, if I'm brutally honest. But there you have it. It appears that my size-six feet (seven in trainers) are online stars, whether I like it or not.

The reason I'm not a fan of my toes is because they're reeeeeeeally looooooooong. They always have been – ever since the rest of me was small, in fact. They're sort of like fingers on my feet. Some people even call them finger-toes. (Rude.) On the plus side, they're quite agile. I bet I could play the piano with them if I tried. Or even type. Or pick up a pen and write in this diary. What if

ELLA TOONE

I'm actually excellent at tightrope-walking and don't even realize it?!

Because my toes are so long, when it comes to wearing heels, there's a clear and ever-present danger of toe cleavage (when the gaps between my toes can be seen). I'd rather not advertise the fact that my toes are longer than pretty much everyone else's, so I avoid anything too low-cut at the front. Usually I go for mules, because they don't just cover most of my feet – they hide three-quarters of my toes too. I've learned a top tip from real-life fashion models, so if I ever do wear sandals, I've got a special trick. Just before someone takes a photo, I crunch up my feet, which magically makes my toes look smaller. Sounds weird, I know, but it works.*

I know this all seems VERY ODD, but after listening to the team chatting in the changing room today, it sounds like everyone gets wound up about something – whether it's their nose or their hair or their earlobes or their eyebrows. There's always something. And what winds me up is my feet.

At the end of the day, my toes and feet seem to be reasonably good at kicking a ball. So even if they do look a bit weird, I suppose I can put up with them.

––––––––––––

* In case you're worrying about my toes, I uncrunch my toes after a photo, obviously. I wouldn't be able to walk like that and there's no way on earth I could play football!

ELLA TOONE

PRE-MATCH BUILD-UP ▷▷

It's our first match in a few days.

I was asked the other day if I get nervous before going out on to the pitch for a big match, and the honest answer is no. Maybe it's because I've done it so much now and I'm confident that I'm fit and have prepared as much as I can. And by the time kick-off finally arrives, I'm excited more than anything else. In fact, I'm BUZZING.

But way back when I was first playing for Manchester United, there were SO many silly things that I felt I absolutely had to do before every match. They were my pre-match rituals. And if I didn't do them, I was SURE that we'd lose. Each season that comes, I give myself a talking to and try to get rid of a few, as deep down I know they aren't REALLY what makes us win or lose.

For starters, there was this chant that I sang the morning of EVERY match day. It went like this:

Woke up this morning, feeling fine

Got Man United on my mind . . .

After a while, I did start wondering how that was actually helping me when I was on the pitch, and I decided it wasn't at all. So I thew that ritual out of the window.

I know a lot of other players have their own rituals that they do before games – and if they can't do them, they think they're going to play badly. For example, I know that Less always puts her left sock on and then her right sock, then her left boot on and then her right boot. And she always jumps in the air seven times before the whistle blows.

Me? I like to eat the same pre-match meal. So I'll have a bagel with eggs and beans, and I'll neck a glass of orange juice. And now I wear my sports bra with the heart sewn into it, just so that I know my dad's there when I'm playing.

Then, just as the ref blows the whistle before kick-off, I'll shout, 'Come on, girls! Straight in!' Every time.

THINGS I LIKE AND THINGS I DON'T

I'm going to write down some of my favourite and worst things in the world right now. I'm curious to see how these things change over time, and wonder if I'll read back over my diary in ten years and think, *Ella, you haven't changed AT ALL!* or, *Wow, you were WEIRD back then.*

My favourite musicians

- ABBA

- Elton John

- Bee Gees

- Lionel Richie

- Coldplay

Things that wind me up

- London – I mean, it's not Tyldesley, is it?

- Jet lag – eating Skittles at 4am because I can't sleep and there's no other food in the hotel room is NOT my idea of fun

- Los Angeles – because of the jet lag

Things I love

- Playing for England

- Tyldesley

- Flapjacks

- Playing in the rain

- Cheesecake (but if there's no cream on the side, forget it)

ON THE ORIGINS OF SOCCER

I'm sitting here waiting for treatment – honestly, our physios are THE BEST – and I decided that rather than muck about on TikTok, I'd write about a fascinating football fact I just discovered instead, all because of Less.

ELLA TOONE

Way back in 2020, Less said the S word. I was floored. I nearly booked an appointment to get my ears syringed on the spot. Instead of saying 'football' . . . Less said 'soccer'.

To be fair, it was just after she got back from the USA, so I should cut her some slack. Over there, 'football' means American football, which is an entirely different game – more like rugby, but with shoulder pads, face masks and a lot of group hugs. To avoid getting confused, they call our sort of football 'soccer' instead.

But the thing is, I did a bit of research and – believe it or not – it turns out that the word 'soccer' was actually invented, guess where . . . ?

In the UK!

It was way back in the 19th century. Apparently, students at the University of Oxford wanted to find a way to stop people getting mixed up between rugby (because the full name for rugby is actually 'rugby football') and football (officially called 'association football'). So they lost the 'by' of rugby, added a 'g' and popped an 'er' on the end to make it . . . RUGGER.

Shortening association football was trickier. They tried out 'assoc-er' but decided that it sounded weird, so they mucked about with the spelling, lost the 'a' at the beginning, got rid of an 's' as well, doubled the 'c' and added another 'er' to make . . . SOCCER. (And if you've managed to read all of that without totally scrambling your brain, award yourself three points for the win.)

Basically, the British invented the word 'soccer' and then forgot they did and started calling it 'football' instead.

Anyway, Less has gone back to saying it the right way now, so we're good.

THE BIT YOU DON'T SEE

As part of our analysis sessions, footballers rewatch quite a lot of matches. For the record, this isn't *just* to yell, 'LOOK AT THAT GOAL! HOW BRILLIANT WERE WE IN THAT GAME???!' (Though I have to admit that sometimes it would be rude not to . . .) It's also a top way of figuring out which strategies work best, what we've done well and what didn't go so well and we should probably never do again if we can help it.

Anyway, we were rewatching matches today in advance of our upcoming games and doing all of the above, when I suddenly realized that there's a part of the match that no one sees on telly – what we do BEFORE we get to the tunnel.

So here's the inside scoop – EVERYONE DOES SOMETHING DIFFERENT.

Some people go out on to the pitch before the game just to soak up the atmosphere.

Some never do.

Some put their kit on right away.

Some leave it until about two minutes before they need to be out on the pitch to get their gear on.

ELLA TOONE

Some listen to the music playing on the changing-room speakers.

Some have earphones in because they'd rather listen to their own far superior tunes, thanks very much.

Some channel Rapunzel and give themselves a bazillion plaits.

Some go for the always-popular high ponytail. (That's me, that is.)

Some people don't talk to anyone.

SOME DO NOT SHUT UP.

But however a player prepares, by the time we've run through the tunnel and out on to the pitch, we're not different at all. We're part of a team, and we all want the same thing.

We want to win.

KEEP ON SMILING

It's been pretty full-on at training this week, with drills by the million (at least). So this afternoon, the coach suggested we pop into town for a breather.

Can you believe that, within about seven minutes of us arriving, the paps (short for paparazzi – they're photographers who try to get photos of us doing normal or – if they're REALLY lucky – totally embarrassing stuff) had found us? I mean, really? These guys are relentless. I totally get that they're just doing their job, and that all they want is to get a good picture and sell it to the highest bidder, but I got papped eating a pasty in Tyldesley once . . . who wants to see a photo of that? Not me.

But it means that I can't relax in public. Because you can 100 per cent guarantee that if I frown for a millisecond or look even the tiniest bit narked about something, then faster than you can say 'cold pasty', it'll be all over the internet that Ella Toone is having A Really Bad Day.

So here's my genius solution: if the paparazzi are anywhere near, I smile all the time. And I mean ALL the time. Even if I'm talking about the weather. Or if that goal last week should actually have been disallowed because no way was it off-side. Or how gutted I was when they discontinued Tooty Frooties.

As a result, I like to think I'm pretty good now at being stern while looking as if I just scored a goal in extra time. That keeps the paps quiet.

TO HUG OR NOT TO HUG, THAT IS THE QUESTION

Let's talk about hugs.

Some people hug all the time, while some people never do. Me? I can take or leave them (and usually I'll leave them). I wouldn't say I NEVER hug – I don't mind hugging – but I'm definitely less of a hugger than, say, Less. She LOVES a hug.

I do have a few exceptions to my not-too-many-hugs-thanks policy. If any of these things happen, then I might cave and give one or two people a squeeze:

1. If I score.

2. If someone else on my team scores.

3. If we win a game.

Actually, there is just one more . . .

4. If we win the Euros.*

When this happens, I hug absolutely EVERYONE. Twice!

---

* This happened in 2022, in case I haven't mentioned that enough yet.

AYE, AYE, CAPTAIN!

I was feeling a little stressed out about the upcoming tournament this morning, thinking about how many people would be watching us, both in the stadiums and on telly around the world. I decided to have a chat with our amazing captain, Leah, and she totally sorted me out with her straight talking. She basically told me to focus on the football.

The thing about Leah is that not only does she say it how it is, but she's incredibly kind with it. You know that she means everything she says, and then once you've spoken about the serious stuff, she'll make you laugh until your sides hurt. She's GREAT.

I met Leah at one of my first camps and found out

right away that she's easy to get on with. She makes you feel welcome, and you can just tell that she's a proper leader. She leads by example and inspires everyone to want to win.

I remember after the 2022 Euros, Leah gave us the BEST advice. Obviously, the press were all over us like a rash, so we couldn't do ANYTHING without the paparazzi taking photos. But Leah reckoned that we had two weeks' grace after winning. During that time, we could let our hair down and do pretty much whatever we liked – basically I could've danced until 4 a.m. dressed as a lobster, and no one would've minded because we'd won the Euros – but after that two weeks, normal service would resume. And she was right!

The celebrations straight afterwards were EPIC. Over the summer, while we'd been bonding as a team, our families had been doing *exactly the same thing*, so it was nice for them to celebrate together too. The after party was A-M-A-Z-I-N-G. It was like a wedding, really, and there was even a cake! We were all there with our families on the dancefloor together. It was a really, REALLY special night.

Then I went straight to Ibiza and to the most amazing club that people call a 'musical wonderland', with a poolside stage and open-air dancefloor! I watched the DJ Calvin Harris* perform and that was just AMAZING.

---

*Podcast fans, this is Vick Hope's actual husband! How sick is that?!

I loved it. Ibiza is one of my favourite places, and Leah was absolutely right – as always! No matter what we got up to, no one back home minded. After all, we'd just won the Euros, hadn't we? (I did mention that, right?)

I ♥ POTATOES

I had seriously the BEST jacket potato ever for tea tonight. It was light and fluffy, with the crispiest skin, and inside there was butter melting and a pile of baked beans on top. I had a salad with it, and it was all DELICIOUS.

As footballers, we love CARBS. Carbohydrates – starchy foods like potatoes, pasta, rice, bread and cereals – are a great source of energy. We all need them for a balanced diet, and footballers need them for fuel, especially when we're training or on match days.

Leah Williamson's favourite carb is BREAD. She's a bit fussy, so sometimes I've seen her eat four slices of toast for breakfast. That's JUST toast with nothing on it. I know. Weird.

Less's favourite carb is PASTA. Not on its own though – with LOADS of sauce.

Mine's POTATOES, obviously. I like bread, don't get me wrong. But if I have it at the start of a meal, when I'm really hungry, I sometimes can't stop myself from eating ALL the bread. Then – disaster! – I can't eat my main meal, which might have potato in it. And I definitely don't want to miss out on that!

ELLA TOONE

OUTRAGEOUS!

We played a game tonight of 'Who's Most Likely To?'. How it works is someone suggests a category – like 'most likely to sleep through a match' or 'most likely to eat an entire sharing bag of crisps on their own' – and then we vote who on the team would win that award.

And Less and I were labelled as the pair most likely to thieve! Actually, it's worse than that. They said that Less would be the one distracting everyone, and I'm the one mostly likely to do the robbing!

RUDE.

And they're so wrong! If I'm such a thief, how do

they explain the time that MY boots went missing? I don't know who did it. Probably Georgia or Keira – one of them. But why is no one saying *they* are the most likely to thieve?!

Though I suppose Less has got form . . . when she was at Arsenal, she admits to pinching one of Beth Mead's boots, just as a prank. (If you're a footballer, take it from me – your boots are the LAST things you want to lose!) But Less says that she felt so guilty that she immediately gave them back again.

Anyway, I've made a decision. As MOST LIKELY TO BE A THIEVING DOUBLE ACT isn't actually an accolade worth shouting about, I've decided to look at it from a more positive angle. I reckon what my lovely teammates are really saying is that Less and I are MOST LIKELY TO WORK AS A TEAM TO GET STUFF DONE.

There. That's much better.

I DON'T DO SMALL TALK

You know when you meet people for the first time, and it's polite to ask them questions like 'How are you?' and chat about where they're from, what the weather is like, what sort of sandwich filling they like and so on?

Well, I'm no good at it.

I'm thrown into those situations all the time these days, so I should have learned how to deal with it by now. There were some bigwigs visiting the training camp this morning, and they came round and chatted with the players. That's when I really should have piled in with, *'Hello there, Important Person. It's lovely to meet you. Can I ask, do you think that pineapple on pizza is a super idea or an abomination?'* (Or something like that. You know, a casual question to launch a conversation with a total stranger.) But I couldn't. I felt too nervous and awkward to say anything. If I've never met a person, I clam up tighter than, well, a clam.

The only time I don't struggle with talking to new people is when a new player joins the team. They walk into the dressing room and – BOOM – they fit in straight away. It's like we've known each other for ever.

And when I know someone *really* well, it's a totally

different story. No clamming up over here. I can talk for England.

PEOWWWWWWW!

What. A. Day. As a break from training, Leah suggested that we headed out and did some actual team building, and the activity she planned was . . . NERF GUNS. Whoooooop!

We basically fired trillions of little water pellets at each other. And I can exclusively reveal that they really do hurt quite a bit when someone blasts them at you. So my basic tactic was to hide on the floor, using everyone else as a human shield. (Genius, right?)

All the girls were ganging up on the staff

members, which we NEVER do in real life. I love how it totally flipped the group dynamic! Suddenly us Lionesses came together and, for one afternoon only, WE WERE IN CHARGE!

Here's another thought that occurred to me when I was avoiding those pesky bullets . . . when you have such a big team of people, everyone is so different. For some people, having a conversation might be completely out of their comfort zone, while shooting Nerf guns at my head might be something they LOVE. And at the same time, some people might prefer to sit around chatting or playing cards rather than being pelted with water pellets!

I know what everyone's like on the pitch, but fling them into a totally alien situation and you get to

ELLA TOONE

see a whole new side to them. Team bonding is the best thing EVER.*

PERFECT PLAYLISTS

I was chatting with Leah today, and we reckon we've got the same taste in music. We like the kind of music that you'd hear at a sixtieth birthday party! Plenty of old stuff, some newer hits . . . you know, songs that EVERYONE knows and can sing along to. I'm all over that sort of playlist – just NOT the country stuff that Leah likes. (Unless it's 'Islands in the Stream', of course.)

Music's SO important to the Lionesses. In the

---

* Ideally, as long as you're not being shot in the head.

dressing room and at camp it can REALLY lift the mood. Leah's very keen to tap into that. She reckons that music changes everything – especially after a loss, when everyone sits in sorrow in the changing room. So that's when she tries to cheer everyone up and get things moving again – with music.

But what to play?!

Leah says that you can go a couple of ways. You can play a heartfelt ballad by Adele and make everyone cry. It sounds weird, but that could be just what we all need to let our emotions out. Then, after singing along and/or bawling our eyes out, we might be ready to pick ourselves up again.

Or you can go more upbeat with ABBA and pop

ELLA TOONE

on 'Does Your Mother Know?' Or, maybe 'Voulez-Vous'! There's something about an ABBA song that lifts people's spirits, even after losing a football match. Leah thinks 'Unwritten' by Natasha Bedingfield is another TOP TUNE for cheering you up when you're down. (And I have to admit that she's right.)

Meanwhile, Less has a really cool theory. She says that there are songs that you hear every now and again, but especially when you're having a REALLY GOOD TIME and they lodge in your brain. So if you're down when you next hear them, it reminds you of the good times and instantly picks you back up and gets you feeling good again.

Basically, music rocks. (Unless it's country.)

PARCELS FROM HOME

Awwwwwww. Joe has just sent me THE most awesome poster! It's HUGE. He's plastered it with pictures of all my family and friends, with a little note from each of them.

It reminds me of the MAHOOSIVE book he made for me to take to Australia for the World Cup in 2023. I love getting phone calls and messages from my family when I'm at training camp, but when it's a longer trip, they become even more important to me. And when we set off for Australia, we didn't know how long the trip was actually going to be because we didn't know how long we'd be in the tournament. As soon as a team is knocked out of a tournament, they go home. We had no idea that we'd make it to the final!

ELLA TOONE

We arrived two weeks before the tournament because there's such a massive time difference between the UK and Australia. So first we had to get over the jet lag. (Ah, jet lag. I love jet lag.*) And reaching the final meant that we were there for SIX WEEKS in total!

Joe had put together a huge book filled with really nice messages from my family and friends about how proud they were of me. It was SO thoughtful. I read it all the time, especially on nights when we had a match the next day, and I'd cry at the messages because they made me feel SO proud and SO happy.

---

* I really don't.

WATER, WATER, EVERYWHERE

I already know that this is probably TMI (Too Much Information), but if you're a wannabe scientist or nutritionist or just interested in the mechanics of the human body, you'll be totally fascinated! (There's also a reasonable chance that you'll go *ewwwwwwwwww*, but I can live with that.)

I can't wee for AGES after a match.

See? Fascinating.

I think it's because I sweat so much – I run over 10 km during a 90-minute match, which is the same as running from one end of the pitch to the other 95 times. So by the end I'm totally dehydrated. This wouldn't be a problem under normal circumstances – you'd just have a drink of water and rehydrate your body slowly. But what you might not know is that as soon as we've gone back down the tunnel, we have to do a wee test so the match officials can make sure we haven't taken any medicines that will make us perform better (that would be dangerous . . . and cheating). So unless I make sure to drink LOADS of water straight after a game, the wee test can take a stupidly long time.

After the 2022 Euros final, we were all singing and dancing round the changing room with the trophy in the middle, and suddenly I realized Less wasn't there. It turned out SHE was trying to produce a sample of wee and couldn't! She was so empty after the match that it seemed to take

HOURS. But she rocked up eventually, and that was another excuse to go wild again!

So basically, if you're a footballer – or someone who does exercise of any kind – make sure that you DRINK ENOUGH WATER. You often don't even realize how dehydrated you are!

According to experts, if someone faints during a match, one of the most common reasons is dehydration. Apparently, if a player doesn't drink enough, they become SO exhausted that they pass out. It's even worse if they're running fast. So I try to drink as much as I can, and if it's warm, I drink even more. Don't get me wrong: I don't neck so much water that I'm sloshing around like a washing machine on the woollens cycle. But I'd rather drink water than go down like a sack of spuds on the pitch.

ELLA TOONE

AND THE MEDAL FOR BEST PHOTO OF THE EUROS 2022 GOES TO . . .

There are some girls who take ages to do their hair in the changing room and use loads of products to make sure their hairstyle stays in for the whole match. Less likes to spend a while on her hair, and she wears make-up too.

My look is super low maintenance. It only takes me about a minute to put my hair in a high ponytail before a game. I don't worry about plaits or doing anything too fancy – I just pull it back and *ta-daaaaaaaa*! And I don't bother with make-up – I usually just put some moisturizer on my face. Mascara isn't an issue either because my lashes are always ready to go! But either way, I NEVER want to look as if I just fell out of bed and on to the pitch because there are sports photographers EVERYWHERE.

Sports photographers are SO good at capturing the best sporting moments – the action, the skill, the emotion, the tears, the joy, the skidding-on-your-knees-across-the-pitch-after-a-stonking-goal – that type of thing. And then there are the photos that accidentally capture the funniest moments for ever. If there's one photo of the entire Euros that deserves a medal, it's this . . .

We were on the stage after winning, and everyone was celebrating. I think it was probably when Leah lifted the trophy that we all jumped up into the air together. But when she jumped up, Less's medal flew up and SMACKED her . . . right in the eye! And THAT's the moment the photographers caught on film. It's brilliant!

Euros medals are quite heavy, and Less told me afterwards – more than once, actually – that it really hurt when it whacked her. Plus she's fairly sure that there's an eyebrow-shaped dent* in her medal. But luckily, she's even more sure that it didn't ruin the moment.

I mean, how could it? We'd just won the Euros!**

_____

* Fun fact! Euros medals are very easy to damage. Leah's has toothmarks all round the outside and mine has been properly bashed up too. But it shows they've been won and worn, so I'm pretty sure I can put up with a bit of wear and tear.
** Not entirely sure I've mentioned that yet, so popping it in to be on the safe side.

THE NOT-SO-SECRET DIARY OF A FOOTBALLER

DID YOU KNOW . . .?

After the Euros in 2022, the band Coldplay celebrated our win by writing the names of all the Lionesses on their drum.* REALLY. They were on their Music of the Spheres World Tour, and they invited me and Less to come and watch them perform at Wembley on 22 August 2022. It was one of the best concerts we've EVER been to. We knew ALL the words.

---

* I've thought about this a lot and it must've been either a very big drum or very small writing.

ELLA TOONE

JUST CALL ME ELLA 'FIVE PIES' TOONE

I haven't written about my feet for a few days, so let's sort that out right away. Actually, I'm going to write about feet and PIES. Because I once joked that I could balance five pies on my weak foot* if I wanted to.

Why?

---

* Just for the record, when I say 'weak', I don't mean that one of my feet is weak and feeble or anything. It's still perfectly capable of playing football. It's just that if I had to choose a foot for hoofing a ball into the back of the net from the halfway line, it wouldn't be that one. It would be my right foot.

THE NOT-SO-SECRET DIARY OF A FOOTBALLER

1. For starters, as you now know, my feet are quite big, so I've got plenty of room for pies on top of them.

2. My weak foot (that's the left one) is half a size bigger than my other foot, so there's EVEN MORE ROOM.

3. As far as I know, no one else has done this, so I figured it was about time someone had a go.

4. I like pies.

I never thought I'd actually have to DO it, of course. I was just sounding off, like I usually do. But I was called out during an interview and presented with a bunch of pies, so I had to give it a go . . .

And I totally did it! I'm officially a five-pie-foot-balancing champion.

THE LOBSTER

Get ready for definitely the most valuable piece of advice in this whole diary.

IF you ever go to a team BBQ with the rest of the Lionesses, and **IF** someone suggests that it would be a really great idea for everyone to pull each other's names out of a hat, and **IF** (yes, I'm still going – this is going to be a very long sentence) the person who pulls your name out then has the chance to choose a fancy dress outfit for you, and

THE NOT-SO-SECRET DIARY OF A FOOTBALLER

IF the person who picks your name is Mary Earps . . . then I strongly suggest that you IMMEDIATELY RUN AWAY. Because once you wriggle your way into whatever ludicrous outfit that Mary's chosen for you, you won't be going *anywhere*.

In case you haven't worked it out, this happened to me.

I, Ella Toone, had to dress up in an inflatable lobster costume, tastefully paired with leopard-print heels. I was sweating so much, it was like a sauna in there! My face turned the actual shade of lobster red, and the suit was so puffed up that I couldn't even reach my burger on the BBQ. AND every time I moved, I got a heel stuck in the decking and nearly ended up flat on my face! (To be fair, I was pretty much a walking airbag, so in the event of an accident, I would've bounced straight back up again.)

What did Mary Earps and literally everyone else do while I was staggering around, getting my heels stuck and going bright red?

They nearly wet themselves laughing, that's what.

THE THING I MOST LOOK FORWARD TO AFTER A TOURNAMENT

I love my bed. It's SO unbelievably comfy.

Being a footballer involves a lot of travel and sleeping in so many different hotel beds. Every night, I feel a bit like Goldilocks (but without the bears, obvs – being a footballer might be a total fairytale, but I don't want to be in a REAL one). Some beds are so firm that they're like sleeping on top of a table. And I can't be doing with soft beds – they're like quicksand. You just sink into the middle of them and vanish. Meanwhile, some have a good level of squishiness and make me want to sleep for a week.

At the end of the day, though, NONE of them are quite like my own bed.

That's just right.

ELLA TOONE

IN THE FUTURE

Two days to go until the tournament kicks off! It's at BIG moments like this when I can't help thinking about the future and what I'll do when I retire – which, just for the record, isn't ANY time soon because I love playing too much even to THINK about stopping. Can you imagine? What else could I do?! Launch my own turbo lashes? Advertise banks on the telly? Design an exclusive range of bucket hats with cool quotes on them? (Actually, that doesn't sound too bad. I might keep that one on the back burner . . .)

One thing I know I want to do is learn another language. I even know which one I'm going to speak.

THE NOT-SO-SECRET DIARY OF A FOOTBALLER

Spanish. (Or should I say Español?)

I learned it at school and I can still remember some of it. So when I'm not quite so busy playing football, I'm going to give it another go. Just think . . . it would be so helpful in Ibiza!

But there's no way I ever want to stop being involved with football completely. So I suppose, when the time is right, the best option would be switching over to become a football manager. A lot of players do this once they're a little more *mature*, let's say. (And that's something else I'm not yet. I'm far too much of a kid still.) People like Franz Beckenbauer, Gareth Southgate, Zinedine Zidane and the one and only Sarina Wiegman have all swapped from being on the pitch to being on the sidelines. Former players know what they're talking about because they've

ELLA TOONE

played themselves. So I like to think that I might be able to give that a go. Obviously, I'd need to develop my management style, but I've already got a pretty good idea of two key instructions I'd like to give to my team:

1. Don't worry about defending. Just ATTACK.

2. I don't care if we concede five, AS LONG AS WE SCORE SIX.

I might need to fine-tune these tactics a little . . .

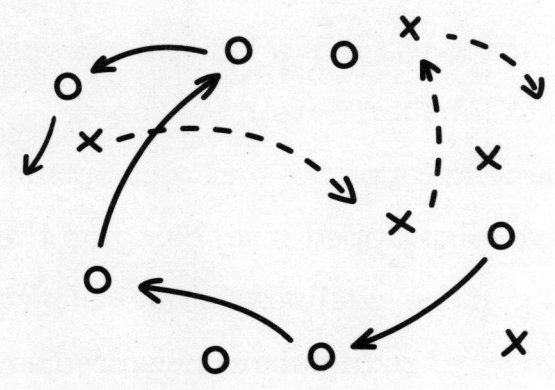

THE BEST FINAL WHISTLE EVER

A quick quiz!

What's the name of the whistle mostly used by referees worldwide?

1. Valkyrie.

2. Valkeen.

3. The Roy Keane.

Answer on the next page *

ELLA TOONE

A whistle is something that you hear a LOT during a match. It starts play at the beginning of the first AND second halves, AND extra time, AND after a goal. And it stops play for a free kick or a penalty, AND at the end of each half, AND to signal about a gazillion other things. But the best whistle of all (if you're winning) is the final whistle, which tells everyone that the game is officially over.

As it's the first match of the tournament

---

* The answer is 2. A Valkeen whistle has a fancy flip mechanism, which means a referee can hold the whistle in the palm of their hand, ready to whip it up at a moment's notice to *PEEEEEEEP* at a foul. The Valkeen has a very high-pitched sound, designed to travel a looooooong wayyyyyyyy.

tomorrow, to get ourselves all fired up and ready to go, the Lionesses spent today reminiscing about our best final whistle of all time. It was the last *peeeeeeeeep* of the Euros (did I mention we won in 2022?), and a moment I'll remember FOR EVER . . .

The score was England 2 – Germany 1. We were so close to victory. It was near the end of extra time, but it didn't matter – we couldn't let our guard down for a second. We were still playing to win. And here is where my memory turns into glorious Technicolor™. It's like being at the cinema IN MY HEAD.

Less and I were on the right-hand side of the pitch. Less was chasing the ball, I was behind her and, in that instant, we heard it.

The final whistle.

ELLA TOONE

I've never felt that many emotions in one second. I was happy. I was crying. I'd jumped into the air and was hugging Less. It was surreal. But at the same time, it was actually REAL. The final whistle meant that we'd won . . . and not just that game but the whole tournament.

We'd won the UEFA Women's Euros 2022.

We were the actual winners!

WE'D BROUGHT FOOTBALL HOME.

I'm not crying. *You're* crying.

And now, with the first match of this tournament just one sleep away, I can't help but dream of what it would be like to win again. The emotions. The interviews. The events. The news reports.

THE NOT-SO-SECRET DIARY OF A FOOTBALLER

The murals. The knowledge that all our hard work has paid off. There truly is no greater feeling.

After we won the Euros in 2022, there was this sudden explosion of FAME . . . Everyone wanted to know about the England Women's team. It was WILD. We'd been in such a bubble during the tournament that we hadn't seen the impact we'd been having in the real world. It took us all by surprise. I think it was when people came up to me at the airport for autographs and pictures when I got back that it really hit me. We really had done something massive.

Fame is the weirdest thing. Before the Euros, we could just get on with playing football and no one cared. Now we're under such scrutiny all the time. Everyone wants to know where we're going, what we're doing, and all about our personal lives . . .

I didn't expect that, and it's REALLY full on. I don't mind admitting that I struggled with it for a while, but I like to think that I'm pretty good at coping with it now.

The way I look at it is that everyone is just chuffed to bits we're doing well. Our fans are SO happy. They're delighted to have something to celebrate, and when they come and say hi in a supermarket or the street, they're just sharing their excitement. Sometimes it might get a tiny bit intrusive – say if someone wants an autograph when I'm getting my nails done. (On a practical level, I can't even pick my nose when I'm at the nail bar – how I'm going to sign an autograph is beyond me.) But on the whole, our fans are very understanding and incredibly cool. Actually, who am I kidding?

WE HAVE THE BEST FANS IN THE WORLD!!!

And the upside to the fame is that everyone is SO much more interested in women's football now. People are talking about it and investing more money in the game than ever before. It's great to know that we might have inspired a whole new generation of female footballers. Because of us, they can see that dreams DO come true, and in a few years, it might be them – or even YOU – holding the trophy.

THE BIT AT THE END WHERE I WRAP EVERYTHING UP

The wait is over. The opening match is tomorrow, and we'll soon put all the training into practice. I'm nervous, but I'm buzzing too. Because there's something that I already know, and so does every other Lioness at this England camp: *bonding off the pitch makes you so much stronger on it.*

There's a totally unbreakable bond that all the Lionesses share. We've trained together, we've laughed together and we've worked hard together. And tomorrow we're going to go out there and do our very, very, VERY best to win together.

Tomorrow, I'm going to remember what my dad would always say.

'Get stuck in, enjoy yourself and show your skills.'

Thanks, Dad. I will.